Birmingham
& the Black Country
cycle
Rides

Published and printed by: Haynes Publishing, Sparkford,
Yeovil, Somerset BA22 7JJ.

British Library Cataloguing-in-Publication Data:
A catalogue record for this book is available
from the British Library.

ISBN 1 84425 007 5

Birmingham
& the Black Country
cycle
Rides

Nicky Crowther

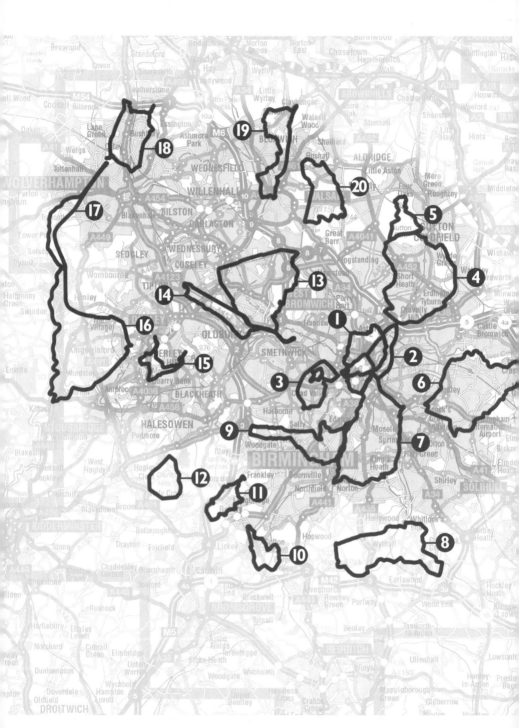

CONTENTS

		Grade	Distance	Page
	Introduction			**6**
	THE RIDES	**Grade**	**Distance**	**Page**
1	Birmingham sightseeing	easy-moderate	14.5km	**14**
2	Birmingham central canals figure-of-eight	moderate	17km	**22**
3	Edgbaston Reservoir, Harborne Walkway and the Two Towers	easy	11km	**28**
4	North Birmingham green circuit, via Sutton Park and Spaghetti Junction	moderate	20km	**32**
5	Sutton Park Scamper	moderate	11km	**38**
6	East Birmingham green circuit, via the airport	easy	22.5km	**42**
7	South Birmingham green circuit	easy-moderate	22.5km	**50**
8	Country lanes from Earlswood to Forhill and back via Hollywood	easy-moderate	22.5km	**58**
9	Bourn Brook and the River Rea, round the University and Bournville	moderate	21km	**64**
10	Lickey Hills quickie	moderate	10km	**72**
11	Waseley Hills and Frankley Beeches	moderate-difficult	10.5km	**76**
12	Clent Hills	moderate-difficult	9.6km	**80**
13	Sandwell Valley Country Park and canal circuit	moderate	20km	**84**
14	New and Old Main Line canal tour	easy-moderate	20km	**92**
15	Dudley Canals, from Windmill End to the Waterfront	easy-moderate	14.5km	**100**
16	Kingswinford rail trail and Stourbridge Canal	moderate	26km	**108**
17	Valley Park to Wombourne rail trail and canal tour	easy-moderate	18km	**114**
18	North Wolverhampton green circuit	moderate	14.5km	**118**
19	Walsall and the Curly Wyrley	easy-moderate	16km	**124**
20	Barr Beacon and the Rushall and Daw End canals	moderate	13.5km	**130**

Introduction

There is a surprising amount of green leisure riding in Birmingham and the Black Country – if you know where to find it. This book sniffs out 234km (135 miles) of towpaths and parkland which can free you from traffic and show you scenic treasures without leaving the city.

Without the renowned canal network the riding would be much diminished. And what a network it is – full of historical features, and providing access to all corners of the region. In truth, our rides are suggestions only. Arm yourself with the *Birmingham Canal Navigations* map and discover unlimited opportunities for exploration. Two fascinating routes in this book stand out: the New and Old Main Line canal circuit (14) and Dudley Canals (15).

In Birmingham city centre, a wealth of sights and character opens up from the saddle on a sightseeing tour (1) and the canal figure-of-eight ride (2). For rural delights, saddle up for the South Birmingham green circuit (7), Kingswinford and Stourbridge (16), and Walsall and the Curly Wyrley (19).

A hard-working cyclist's mind is rarely far from their next pint or cuppa. For the best refreshment spots, try the cafe in Wombourne old station (routes 16 and 17), the canalside pubs on the Earlswood lanes (tour 8), the Samson & Lion pub in Stourbridge (16), the country park visitor centre cafe at Waseley Hills, and the stylish options at Walsall New Art Gallery (19).

Having a strong green tinge, when the rain falls, many of the routes are only for the hardy – with sturdy bikes and knobbly tyres. But in clement weather, the majority are rideable by most people on most types of bike. The aim being to escape from traffic, there is as little road riding as possible on these journeys, which means rough if rideable patches on most routes. But each has been assessed for weather-proofing, leaving you to decide when to ride. Don't think cycling is a summer pastime only. Riding is more dependent on rainfall. Dry winters make for good cycling just as wet summers make for wet, albeit warmer, cycling.

Each route has also been assessed for children and casual rides, according to traffic, hills and roughness. While all the routes travel a circuit (apart from route 15), they also detail self-contained cycling destinations, such as Sutton Park and Sandwell Valley Country Park, so you can use the book as much as a locator as a route guide.

SECURITY

Ride sensibly, aware of risks; for example, not alone after dark on towpaths. People have been attacked and their bikes stolen from them on towpaths, with afternoons and evenings the riskier time of day. Don't stop for anyone you consider suspicious who asks the time.

Take a friend for company and security.

CLOTHING

- Wear loose or cycle clothing that allows freedom of movement.
- If you buy two items of cycling gear, make one a helmet, and the other, a pair of shorts (you can get baggy ones with inserts inside if you don't fancy figure-revealing lycra). They provide cushioning from the saddle and prevent chafing.
- Wear a top that keeps your shoulders and back fully covered, in case of crashes and to prevent sunburn.
- Always carry waterproofs: cycling in cold, wet clothes makes you miserable.
- Wear shades to protect eyes from dust, insects, trail muck and glare.
- Wear gloves or mitts for better grip and to protect against foliage and falls.

EQUIPMENT

- Always wear a helmet. It can prevent and limit brain damage if you hit your head badly. A good fit is essential. The helmet should be snug and move with the scalp if you wiggle your eyebrows, but not tight enough to pinch the sides of your head.
- A helmet that does not fit will not offer adequate protection. A child's head is especially vulnerable, so try to get children and reluctant teenagers into the habit of

The Birmingham Canal Navigation map is a detailed aid for riding the waterways (see Maps and Literature).

wearing one from the start.
- A reflective belt and lights are essential should you run out of daylight or if the weather changes. Ankle bands are particularly good for alerting car drivers to your presence. Kit children out in a full set of reflectors.
- In case of emergencies, take small change and a mobile phone.
- Always carry a puncture repair kit, spare inner tube and bicycle pump.
- A handlebar computer is a useful aid for seeing how far you've ridden, what your current and maximum speeds are, total and trip mileage, and the time.

STOP THIEF!

The majority of bike thefts are opportunist. You leave your machine propped up outside the newsagent and it's gone when you return. So, rule number one is: always lock it up.

Use a solid steel U-lock (only heavy-duty stranded wire cables are as good) and tie the bike to something immovable like a lamp-post, railings or bike stand. Thread the lock through the frame, the back wheel and the removed front wheel. Take off anything else that unclips; lights, pump, water-bottle and, if you are really

diligent, the saddle.

Insure your bike, either as a named item (if it's worth over a few hundred pounds) on a home contents policy, or individually. Take a photo of it and note the frame number.

Have it postcoded at your local police station. Hundreds of recovered bikes a year are never reunited with their owners because police could not trace them.

IN CASE OF ACCIDENT

- Place the rider in the recovery position using the minimum of movement. Keep the rider warm and place a jacket beneath their head for comfort.
- If they have sustained a head injury, do not remove their helmet unless they are bleeding severely.
- Do not give food in case they need to be operated on in a hurry.
- If you have to leave an injured rider to seek assistance, make sure they are warm and feel able to stay awake.
- Make a note of where you have left them on your map and mark the spot with a piece of bright clothing held down by a stone or attached to a tree.
- Get help as quickly as possible.

ROUTES FOR CHILDREN

Children love to cycle and cycling is good for children and their parents.

Birmingham and the Black Country have numerous car-free parks and spaces ideal for little-to-middling children to play around in on their bikes.

Once they are more adventurous and gaining confidence, you can advance to routes with towpaths, which opens up many more opportunities, including full circuits. Each route is graded for children according to how flat, long or rough it is. Also, each hazard or tricky road section has been detailed, so please read the assessment and the disclaimer carefully before setting out.

Supervise children carefully. This is particularly important on towpaths. Tell them to be prepared to dismount quickly when something suddenly comes up, like a low bridge, steep ramp, blind corner or narrow section. On the road, take care, or dismount altogether to turn right, cross busy roads, change lanes or make any manoeuvre which puts you in the way of traffic.

Carry snacks to revive little flagging legs and spirits. Don't over-estimate their stamina. Build in rests and offer encouragement.

We wish you many happy adventures together.

Car-free and easy for all ages:

Edgbaston Reservoir and Harborne Walkway (Route 3)
Sutton Park estate roads (4 and 5)
East Birmingham green circuit in part (including city farm) (6)
Cannon Hill Park and River Rea cycle route (7 and 9)
Sandwell Valley Country Park (13)

For stronger, able children (includes longer waterside rides):

Sutton Park full circuit in dry weather (5)
Main Line circuit (14)
Dudley canals (15)
Kingswinford and Stourbridge (16)
Valley Park and Wombourne (17)
Walsall and the Curly Wyrley (19)

THE OFF-ROAD CYCLING CODE

1 Stay on the trail
Only ride bridleways and byways
Avoid footpaths
Plan your route in advance
Use Explorer/Landranger maps

2 Tell someone where you are going
(and when you expect to be back)
If possible, leave a map of the ride at home

3 Give way to horses
Stop completely for horses – they can take fright and flight
If you do ride past, do it carefully after checking with the rider

4 Give way to walkers
Say 'hello' too!

5 Bunching is harassing
Ride in twos or threes

6 Prevent erosion
Don't skid deliberately

7 Close the gate behind you
(but if it is fastened open, leave it open)
Don't climb walls or force hedges

8 Stay mobile
Wear a helmet
A mobile phone can be a great aid
Carry a First Aid kit
Carry enough food and drink
Pack waterproofs and warm clothes

9 Take pride in your bike
Maintain it before you leave home
Carry essential spares and tools

10 Be tidy
Litter in the countryside is horrible
Guard against fire

11 Keep smiling

Cannon Hill Park is excellent for family cycling.

A challenge! (hilly, off-road):
Lickey Hills (10), Clent Hills (12)

BIKES ARE LEGAL ON BRIDLEWAYS
Rights of way law forbids cycling on footpaths but you can ride on bridleways (according to Section 30, 1968 Countryside Act).

WEATHER AND SEASONS
Weather forecasts (50p per minute)
Central Midlands 09068 232781
East Midlands 09068 232782

MAPS AND LITERATURE
Useful maps for cyclists covering the region:
- Dudley Council (tel: 01384 814189) and Wolverhampton Council (road safety unit tel: 01902 555734) produce free map leaflets of their cycle networks.
- Birmingham Cycling Map (CycleCity Guides, £4.95, from Push Bikes tel: 0121 632 6753).
- The British Waterways Visitor Centre at Gas Street Basin (tel: 0121 632 6845) is a good source of canal literature.
- Birmingham Canal Navigations map (GeoProjects tel: 0118 939 3567, £4.75). This shows the numerous access points and all locks.
- Ordnance Survey Landranger 31 1:50,000 (and corresponding Explorer 1:25,000 maps).
- Sustrans West Midlands Cycle Route (NCN5) (Sustrans info line tel: 0117 929 0888).
- 22 Routes Around Birmingham (Philip's Cycle Tours Series, in book shops or Sustrans info line tel: 0117 929 0888, around £8.99).

CYCLING ON THE CANAL NETWORK
The Waterway Code for Cyclists
British Waterways does its best to keep the waterways in good repair. As more and more people discover the charm and tranquility of the waterways, there are increased risks of conflict and damage to the environment, so please follow the advice below and enjoy your visit to waterways safely.

Permits
- You need a permit to cycle on towpaths, and information telling you which stretches are open to cyclists (such as all the sections on these routes). This is free and available with an information pack from British Waterways Customer Services, Willow Grange Church Road, Watford WD17 4QA (tel: 01923 201120; E-mail: enquiries.hq@britishwaterways.co.uk; website: www.britishwaterways.co.uk).

Look after your waterways
- Avoid cycling where your tyres would damage the path or verges (eg, when they are wet or soft).

Consider others
- Give way to others on the towpath and warn them of your approach. Pedestrians have priority. A polite 'hello' and 'thank you' means a lot.
- Watch out for anglers' tackle and give them

9

time to move it before you pass.
- Dismount under low, narrow or blind bridges.
- Never race one another or perform speed trials.
- It is recommended that you obtain third party liability insurance and equip your bike with a bell or equivalent audible warning.

Take care
- Please dismount alongside locks.
- Access paths can be steep and slippery. Join and leave the towpath with care.
- You must get off and push your cycle beneath low or blind bridges, and where the path is very narrow.
- We strongly advise against cycling on the towpath after dark, but if you have to, use front and rear lights.
- Thorny hedge trimmings can cause punctures. We recommend plastic-reinforced tyres.

Note that the anti-motorbike barriers on towpaths are awkward at the best of times, and are very hard to negotiate with trailerbikes, panniers or recumbents. These barriers occur intermittently.

BIKES ON TRAINS IN BIRMINGHAM AND THE BLACK COUNTRY

Trains and bikes go together like a horse and carriage. Let the train take the strain of getting you and your bike to and from the routes. It's one less car on the roads.

All local trains (Central) carry bicycles free of charge at all times of day throughout the week. For Birmingham timetable and fares enquiries ring the Centro Hotline (tel: 0121 200 2700; website: www.centro.org.uk).

For inter-city trains there are restrictions and charges. Ring National Rail Enquiries for details (tel: 08457 484950).

ORGANISATIONS AND CONTACTS
Push Bikes – the Birmingham Cycling Campaign

Push Bikes is the cycle campaign group for the Birmingham area, and works for the rights and needs of all cyclists in and around the city. They represent the interests of cyclists to European, national and local government, employers and transport providers. Members are kept informed via a quarterly newsletter and regularly updated website, and there's a monthly meeting (the first Tuesday) at the office.

Membership also brings a 10 per cent discount at a number of local bike shops.

Push Bikes also organises leisure rides throughout the year and events during National Bike Week. They link with other cycle groups across Britain through the Cycle Campaign Network. Push Bikes has over 300 members in Birmingham and neighbouring areas, including Solihull and Sandwell.

Contact: 54 Allison Street, Digbeth, Birmingham B5 5TH (tel: 0121 632 6753; E-mail: push.bikes@virgin.net; website either: www.pushbikes.freeserve.co.uk or www.pushbikes.org.uk).

Sustrans in Birmingham and the Black Country

Routes in this book use several excellent sections of the National Cycle Network (NCN) in Birmingham and the Black Country. Clear signposting, low-car or no-car sections and toucan crossings are its hallmarks, creating safe and satisfying through-routes particularly in dense areas, suitable for all ages and abilities. The chances are, if there's a dismantled railway line in your neighbourhood, someone at Sustrans, the charity behind the network, has their eye on it.

The main route in Birmingham and the Black Country is NCN5, the West Midlands Cycle Route, which runs north-south directly through the heart of the city en route between Oxford, Stratford upon Avon and Derby (a total of 260km).

It enters in the southwest at Frankley and follows the course of the River Rea on plenty of parkland almost as far as the centre. It traverses the city centre via New Street Station, Broad Street and Centenary Square then joins the Birmingham & Wolverhampton Main Line Canal beside the National Indoor Arena and heads northwestwards. It enters Sandwell in West Bromwich and leaves the canal in the Galton Valley to cross Sandwell Valley Country Park, running over the M5 and under the M6 motorways. It then heads right through the centre of Walsall, and continues northwards on a rail trail near Rushall and Pelsall, leaving the environs at Brownhills.

A further route between Birmingham and Coventry, taking in the NEC and Birmingham Airport, is under development and due for completion in 2005.

Meanwhile, NCN5 also connects with NCN5A Thames Valley (London to Oxford), NCN6A South Midlands (Oxford to Derby via Leicester) and NCN6B Derby to York.

A detailed map of the full NCN5 is available, along with all other NCN route maps, from the NCN Information Service (tel: 0117 929 0888; website: www.nationalcyclenetwork.org.uk).

The routes in this book that use NCN5 include the South Birmingham green circuit (7), Bourn Brook and River Rea (9), Waseley Hill and Frankley Beeches (11), Sandwell Valley Country Park and canal circuit (13), and the New and Old Main Line Canal circuit (14), as well as the North Wolverhampton green circuit (18).

Sustrans (it stands for 'sustainable transport') works on practical projects to encourage more walking and cycling and reduce motor traffic. The NCN, the charity's flagship project, passes through urban centres and will eventually reach all corners of the country. Over a third of the total 10,000 miles due for completion in 2005 will be traffic-free.

The CTC – Cyclists' Touring Club

This is the national cyclists' organisation, representing cycling interests and running an excellent information service, also a network of long-established recreational district associations who primarily organise leisure rides (tel: 01483 417217; website: www.ctc.org.uk).

Surviving the traffic

Don't let Birmingham's heavy traffic put you off riding around the city. With assertiveness, awareness and a tad of fitness, you can claim your space on the tarmac and enjoy being in control of your journey.

There are bad and careless drivers and good cyclists. The reverse is also true. Safety depends on two factors: awareness of potential hazards and how to avoid them; and considerate cycling techniques designed to catch the attention of other drivers and help them to help you.

Cycling hazards

Left-hand bends
Indicate to request space as you swing round a left-hand bend so you don't get squeezed. Cars tend not to allow for your travel space. Indicate with your right arm.

Gaps in your line of traffic
This can mean space is being left for a car outside your vision to turn into. Brake and approach with great care.

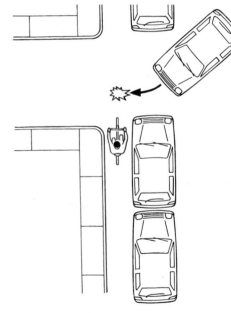

Drafting
Drafting or slipstreaming vehicles is fast, furious fun, so naturally, it is dangerous. Vehicles brake more quickly than bikes, especially in the wet.

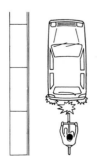

Bollards
These help pedestrians, but hinder cyclists. Anticipate that you may be squeezed, and request space by sticking out an arm in good time.

Car doors opening

*Leave 1m between you and any parked cars.
Catch the driver's eye in their wing mirror.*

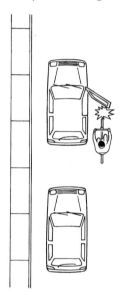

Being crushed by lorries or buses

*Never get on the inside of buses, coaches or
lorries going left. The most frequent cause of
cycling fatalities is a rider being crushed as the
vehicle cuts off the apex of the corner. At lights
wait behind big vehicles, and let them go ahead
around corners.*

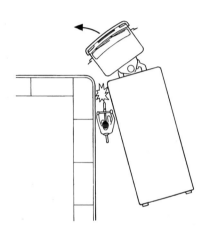

GOOD CYCLING TECHNIQUES

Indicate and communicate

*Use big arm movements in plenty of time to let
drivers react. Make eye contact. Call out. Use a
bell. Thank a helpful manoeuvre with a thumbs-
up or the like.*

Be well lit at night

*Drivers see only lights after dark, not shadows.
Reflective strips are a great aid.*

Be patient and control your temper

*Learning to handle the occasional idiot is part
of becoming a true cyclist.*

Don't be late

*Cycling takes skill, nerve and balance. If you are
worried or late, you are putting yourself at risk.
Keep your mind on the riding.*

Get reasonably fit

*Then you can flow with the traffic, not against it,
get out of small spaces quicker – and enjoy
yourself more.*

Birmingham sightseeing

Discover contrasting gems from Brindleyplace to Aston, including the Jewellery Quarter and the floozie in the jacuzzi.

Short in distance, long on interest; in one afternoon this classic tourist ride spans 400 years. Travel between 17th-century Aston Hall and 21st-century Millennium Point, past buildings and sights which show Brum's persistent commercial and social evolution.

Take your time, and enjoy refuelling as you go, in trendy Brindleyplace, or the Edwardian Tearoom in the Museum & Art Gallery, the alternative Warehouse Cafe in Digbeth or the Woodman pub opposite Millennium Point, or anywhere else that takes your fancy.

This is the only route in the book that's entirely road-based, but there are short sections in the city centre on pedestrianised roads, where you have to walk the bike and give way to pedestrians. They come passing

RIDE INFORMATION

Distance	14.5km (9 miles)
Car-free	1.5km (1 miles) (11%)
Grade	Easy-moderate (a few rises, some busy road junctions)

Suitability for children and occasional riders?
Not really. The traffic levels are still too high for children (but you could use it for a low-car mini-tour, such as from Brindleyplace via Centenary/Victoria Squares to the shopping streets and back).

Traffic
For experienced riders there is only one serious encounter (Curzon Circle), but less experienced riders might prefer to tackle several on foot; Victoria Rd/Lozells Rd, Gt Hampton St, the Jewellery Quarter roads feel confined during office hours, Curzon Circle, Vauxhall Rd, Walter St or Lichfield Rd. Everyone, please take care throughout.

Start/finish
Anywhere en route, perhaps Aston Hall, the Jewellery Quarter or Millennium Point. We use Centenary Square, on Broad Street at the western end of the centre.

Stations
New Street, Snow Hill, Jewellery Quarter, Duddeston, Aston.

Refreshments
The Edwardian Tearoom in the Museum & Art Gallery; the Warehouse Cafe (tel: 0121 633 0261, 54 Allison St, Digbeth, in the same building as Push Bikes and the Cycle Chain bike shop) lies 500m south of Albert St (down Park St); The Woodman and the Old Railway pubs (opposite and just past Millennium Point) are two watering holes renowned for the rock clientele; en route, cafes and pubs are frequent in the centre, but peter out around Heartlands, Nechells and Aston.

Bike shops
Cycle Chain (tel: 0121 643 1500) 54 Allison St, Digbeth (hire service and second-hand. Shares a building with Push Bikes, Friends of the Earth and the Warehouse Cafe.

Top: Set off from Centenary Square, via the Central Library building.

Below: Local children and elderly people designed these community railings in Heartlands.

through the Central Library building, and on the far side of St Philip's Cathedral in Temple Row/Bull St.

The majority of roads carry low-to-middling traffic, with half-a-dozen trickier exceptions (see Traffic), but nothing that cannot be walked around, or, with the exception of Curzon Circle, ridden if you are confident in traffic.

What to see
Let's hope you're taking notes as well as pedalling. . .

For more information contact the Visitor Centre (tel: 0121 693 6300) en route in Victoria Square opposite the Council House.

The Jewellery Quarter (Museum and Cemeteries)
An atmospheric cluster of streets lined with glinting shop-windows and heavy security doors, where small jewellery manufacturers and associated trades continue to work in original buildings. The quarter overlooks two moss-tinged historic graveyards: the Key Hill and Mint Cemeteries, the final resting place for dozens of Birmingham industrialists. For visitors, the Discovery Centre Museum (tel:

0121 554 3598, 75 Vyse St) has preserved the Smith & Pepper jewellery factory exactly as it was the day it closed in 1981, after 80 years of business.

The route makes a mini-tour of the quarter, taking in the 1903 Chamberlain Clock, museum and cemeteries.

St Paul's Church
Inspired by St Martin-in-the-Fields (Trafalgar Square, London), St Paul's was designed by Roger Eykyns and built 1777-79. It is set in an unassumingly elegant square.

The Lanchester playframe commemorates the factory that once stood on the site.

11am-6pm, free admission), the city's new modern art showcase; and the National Sealife Centre (tel: 0121 633 4700, open Mon-Fri 10am-4.30pm, Sat-Sun to 5pm, admission £8.50/£6 adults/children aged 3+).

The vast National Indoor Arena occupies the northwest corner.

Centenary Square

This open pedestrianised square has the Symphony Hall & Convention Centre at its western end and the Repertory Theatre (1971) to the north. The centre is occupied by the much-debated *Forward* group of statues, and the Hall of Memory War Memorial (1923, Portland stone). The Central Library building lies at the eastern end – the ground floor is a right of way used on the route, for cyclists are permitted to walk here.

Chamberlain Square

The route emerges from the walk through the Central Library overlooking Chamberlain Square, site of the magnificent Museum & Art

Brindleyplace

This new trendy waterfront eating and drinking development off Broad Street lies at the heart of Birmingham clubland. Bars and restaurants line the canal banks near the Old Turn Junction, which also happens to be the centre of the national canal network. (From here you can reach all parts of the country by narrowboat). Places to visit include the Ikon Gallery (tel: 0121 248 0708, open Tues-Sun

Below: Glorious Aston Hall predates the modern structures and motorway which surround it.

The Jewellery Quarter contains two historic graveyards, including the mossy Key Hill cemetery shown here.

Gallery (tel: 0121 303 2834, open Mon-Sat 10am-5pm, Sun from 12.30, free admission), connected by bridge to the Gas Hall building. One highlight is the Industrial Gallery, an exceptional High Victorian iron and glass exhibition room.

Eating in the museum's soaring Edwardian tearoom is an event.

In the middle of the square, the Chamberlain Memorial fountain commemorates Joseph Chamberlain, Mayor of Birmingham and MP.

Victoria Square

Dramatic, tiered Victoria Square contains fine civic buildings and sculpture. It is flanked to the southwest by the temple-like Town Hall (Joseph Hansom 1834), and to the northeast by the magnificent Renaissance-style Council House (H. R. Yeoville Thomason 1879).

Here are also the large 'floozie in the jacuzzi' fountain, and Antony Gormley's fine *Iron Man* (1993), brother, perhaps, to the artist's *Angel of the North* at Gateshead.

St Philip's Cathedral

The English Baroque cathedral was created by architect Thomas Archer in 1715, and also occupies a pleasant square.

Millennium Point

The award-winning modern incarnation of a science and discovery museum, the Thinktank at Millennium Point (website: www.thinktank.ac) is one of Birmingham's newest and proudest innovations.

Curzon Street Station

This was the original terminus for the Birmingham-London railway (Philip Hardwick 1838).

Heartlands community features

Beyond the centre in Heartlands, 'defensible areas' have been installed around the base of tower blocks to create gardens and play areas. Among these, at the end of Little Hall Rd, you will find pattern-cut railings designed by local children and pensioners.

Opposite, amid modern housing, is the restored Bloomsbury Library, a Victorian redbrick building where contemporary touches enhance the brightened original interior – take a look if open.

Left: St Paul's church stands in Birmingham's loveliest square.

1 *(See map on p.21) In Centenary Square, pass the Forward statue, and continue in the same direction (northeast) past the war memorial, over the high walk and through the doors of the building ahead, the Paradise Forum shopping mall beneath the Central Library. (The sign means no cycling, but it is all right to walk through here with bikes.)*

Emerge in Chamberlain Square and drop down, with the Museum & Art Gallery on your left, into Victoria Square (Council House, fountain and Iron Man). Stay at the top of the square, and go left in front of the Council House, to Waterloo St (the right of the pair which come in at this corner).

Continue along here to St Philip's Cathedral and turn right (Temple Row West), passing south of the cathedral. Continue for 150m as far as the Bank of Scotland, then dismount and walk straight ahead on the pedestrian street for another 150m. At Bull Street, at the end, turn right and continue to walk to the traffic lights (Corporation St). Remount and go straight ahead downhill, to where the road curves right (High St), then turn left to the traffic lights with Albert St. Turn right into Albert St, and generally continue in the same direction across the main road into Fazeley St/Bartholomew St/Albert St, becoming Curzon St, to Millennium Point. (At time of research, this area was under development, so follow signs to Millennium Point.)

(If doing this route in reverse, you can cycle all the way through from Albert St to Victoria Square, first along High Street and then New Street).

2 *(See map on p.21)Continue from Millennium Point to Curzon St for 500m and Curzon Circle on the ring road. Dismount to cross and go straight ahead into Vauxhall Rd for 800m, then take a side-turning left (where the road bends right), into Little Hall Rd.*

At the end, after 400m, curve round right to the main road, and bend left to the Parkway junction (there are community railings on the apex). Cross at the pedestrian lights to Bloomsbury Library and take the footpath left of the library (Bloomsbury Way) past the housing along into Bloomsbury St. At the end (the Lanchester climbing frame is opposite, slightly

The 'Lanchester' nearby, is a children's climbing frame shaped like the car built in 1895 at the Lanchester car factory that once stood on the site. The first petrol-engine car made in Britain, it was the Ferrari of its day, and makes a plush playframe too.

Lock Gates roundabout
At the junction of Thimble Mill Lane and Lynton Rd, the roundabout has a radial arrangement of lock gates and narrowboat noses, in reference to the Birmingham & Fazeley Canal (which you crossed 100m earlier).

Aston Hall
Birmingham's grandiose Jacobean stately home (tel: 0121 327 0062) is bordered by the Aston Expressway motorway and the Aston Villa football stadium. However, built by Sir Thomas Holte in 1618-35, it was certainly here first.

The grounds form a public park, and the hall plays host to all manner of events.

Note: you can start and finish at any point.

Is it a library? Is it a mansion? No, it's former
Curzon Street Station.

left) then take the first exit at the roundabout into Thimble Mill Lane.

3 Continue across two roundabouts – the second, Lock Gates, follows after crossing the Birmingham & Fazeley Canal – and up to the dual carriageway – Lichfield Rd. Go carefully straight ahead (pedestrian lights) into the cycle lane of Church Road which becomes Church Lane towards the end, and turn left into Queens Rd. Pass beneath the Aston Expressway motorway, and on to Witton Lane, then turn left at the signs into Aston Hall.

4 Head up the hill to the hall, left past the front and continue in the same direction to the roadway. Turn right into Frederick Rd, left into Bevington Rd and at the end of the main road, Victoria Rd, turn right. This road is quite fast and narrow. After 800m, ride carefully straight ahead over the roundabout into Lozells Rd, or dismount and walk. Turn left soon into Wheeler St, heading for Newtown.

Continue to the bottom (750m), where the road bends right, and turn left up the footpath through the open space. Beyond the church, cross at the pedestrian lights, and take the footpath on the far side between the two tower blocks,

Geach House and Rea House. Go left briefly at the end, and right into Great Hampton Row. Continue for 200m, then turn right into Harford St, and then to the main road, Great Hampton Street. Cross carefully on foot if desired, to dogleg left/right up into Hall Street.

5 This is now the Jewellery Quarter (and mini-circuit). Curving right into Warstone Lane continue for 400m to the Chamberlain Clock. Turn right into Vyse Street and continue to the end 500m. Go left, on the (pavement?), Hockley Hill, and first left down short Key Hill. (There is also an alleyway, from between Nos 47 and 48 Hylton Street, then left down Spencer St off Vyse Rd. At the far end, turn right into Key Hill Drive, and left into Key Hill.)

At the bottom of Key Hill, turn left past the petrol station, on the pavement to avoid ring road traffic if desired. The main entrance to Key Hill Cemetery is 150m along. Continue beneath the railway bridge and take the first left, Pitsford St, up beside Mint Cemetery. Back at Vyse St at the top, go right back to the Chamberlain Clock. Turn left again, back into Warstone Lane and after 250m, head right into Caroline St.

6 Continue down to St Paul's Square and the church at the bottom. Follow the one-way traffic clockwise round to the bottom right-hand corner, and exit the square along Brook St. After 75m turn left into Newhall St for 250m, then right into Lionel St, and continue to the grass of Summer Row.

Go straight ahead on the path on the City Ring Cycle Route, and cross Paradise Circus at the lights and zebra crossing. On the far side, dogleg left/right into Cambridge Street. Continue straight ahead for 500m, over the roundabout and down to the bridge over the canal. Follow NCN5 signs left, down to the towpath at Old Turn Junction. Now at Brindleyplace, explore via the bridges and towpaths. Retrace your steps 400m back past the roundabout, then follow the NCN5 sign right, on the shared path into Centenary Square.

Anthony Gormley's Iron Man contemplates a ride on the Christmas carousel in Victoria Sq.

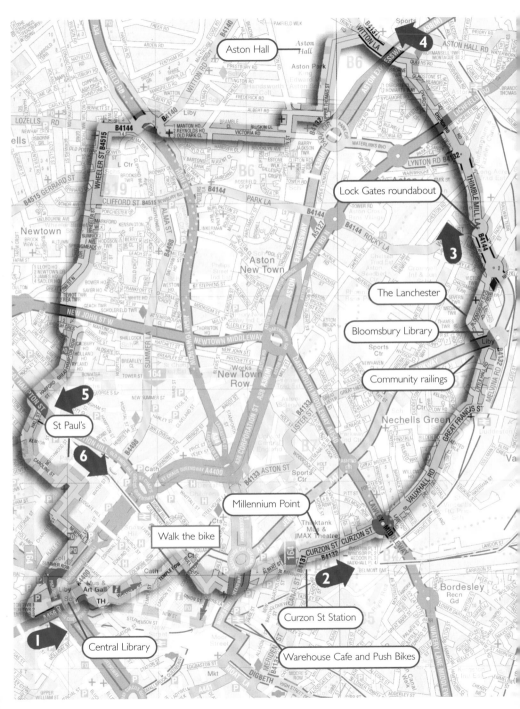

Aston Hall

Lock Gates roundabout

The Lanchester

Bloomsbury Library

Community railings

St Paul's

Millennium Point

Walk the bike

Central Library

Curzon St Station

Warehouse Cafe and Push Bikes

Birmingham central canals figure-of-eight

A simple and fascinating exploration of the city on historic towpaths between Brindleyplace, Gas Street Basin and Spaghetti Junction.

Note: The safety message cannot be over-emphasised. It is compulsory to dismount frequently in places where it is signed. The towpath is awkward and/or popular with other users, and ride with care for yourself and utmost consideration for others. Take a friend for company and security too.

RIDE INFORMATION

Distance	17km (10½ miles)
Car-free	12km (7½ miles) (70%)
Grade	Moderate.

Towpaths on the Digbeth Branch and Birmingham & Fazeley canals (beneath the Telecom Tower around Farmer's Bridge Locks) are full of ins, outs, ups, downs and judders ('kickers' which the horses braced against). It is compulsory to dismount and walk at every lock, and to progress throughout with utmost care for yourself and other users. Also, ride in company to avoid worries about personal safety.

Suitability for children and occasional riders?

This is a difficult call. The ride is an exceptional way to travel around the heart of Birmingham. However, the towpath on the Digbeth Branch and up Farmer's Locks beneath the Telecom Tower is unusually awkward, with blind corners, steep ramps and bumps, and several dismounts are compulsory. Only if you are confident of children's bike control should you take them on this ride – the decision is yours, and they are your responsibility.

Traffic

Minimal, and there are no blackspots. The route follows roads for only 5km, largely on the Central Ring cycle route on quiet roads and estate paths. Watch the lorries through Digbeth backstreets though.

Start/finish

Aston Junction, but anywhere will do. The train is the best way to travel into the centre of Birmingham.

Stations

Birmingham central stations: New Street, Snow Hill and Moor Street, also Duddeston and Aston.

Refreshments

There is a choice of bars at Brindleyplace; the Canalside Cafe at Gas St Basin; the alternative Warehouse Cafe (tel: 0121 633 0261, 54 Allison St, in the same building as Push Bikes and the Cycle Chain bike shop) lies 400m off-route in Digbeth – go left off Milk St up Bordesley St); the Bond cafe on Fazeley St, Digbeth, backing on to the Grand Union Canal.

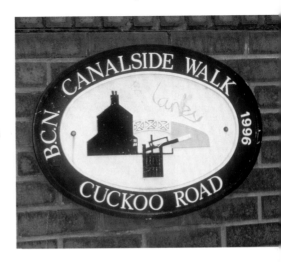

What an intriguing way to access and explore the city centre. The figure-of-eight route for this ride allows you to choose where to start and finish – we choose Aston Junction – but anywhere will do. You could also ride the route in one go, or on successive visits.

Engineering prowess, both industrial age and contemporary, is the feature of the tight city centre towpaths. Especially on the Digbeth Branch (the centrepoint of the '8'), which is now a restored conservation area, and on the Birmingham & Fazeley Canal beneath the Telecom Tower (Farmer's Bridge Locks). The safety message on these cannot be over-emphasised; you must dismount at every lock, at every low bridge and every blind corner. Around the Telecom Tower the towpath is

popular with walkers and joggers, to whom you must give way. The patch around Brindleyplace and Gas Street Basin is also well-walked, and the towpath gets narrow too in places.

Elsewhere, the towpath is well surfaced and drained, but watch also for a narrow section and low bridges on the return leg from Spaghetti Junction along the Birmingham & Warwick Canal. Please follow the Waterways code (see page 11). Note that the anti-motorbike barriers on the towpaths are awkward at the best of times, and very hard to negotiate with trailerbikes, panniers or recumbents. These barriers occur intermittently.

We travel the northern Aston/Heartlands loop clockwise, and southern city centre loop anti-clockwise, running twice along the Digbeth Branch to create an '8'.

Starting on the towpath at Aston Junction (which lies just off the southern end of the Aston Expressway A38(M)), we run northeast up the Birmingham & Fazeley Canal to Spaghetti Junction (Salford Junction), returning on the Birmingham & Warwick Junction Canal to the Grand Union, closing that loop on the Digbeth Branch.

Back at Aston Junction, we now go southwest on the Birmingham & Fazeley Canal as far as Old Turn Junction at

What to see
See Route 1 for places to visit just off the towpaths, including Millennium Point and Aston Hall. Travel directly beneath Spaghetti Junction.

Literature
The Birmingham Canal Navigations map is a good aid to understanding the canals (available from GeoProjects, 9 Southern Court, South St, Reading RG1 4QS, tel: 0118 939 3567, £4.75).

Detailed information leaflets cover The Heartlands Ring describing the top loop; the Birmingham & Fazeley Canal (Walkway Guide No. 1) covering Farmer's Bridge Locks; and the Digbeth Branch Canal (Walkway Guide No. 3) covering the cross-piece of the figure-of-eight. The British Waterways Visitor Centre at Gas Street Basin (tel: 0121 632 6845) is a good source of canal literature.

Bike shops
Cycle Chain (tel: 0121 643 1500) 54 Allison St, Digbeth (hire service and second-hand), in same building as Push Bikes, Friends of the Earth and the Warehouse Cafe.

The canals are signposted just like roads.

Brindleyplace, then pass Gas Street Basin to pick up the Worcester & Birmingham Canal. We leave that soon however, for 5km largely on the Central Ring cycle route, to return for a second pass along the Digbeth Branch Canal and finish at Aston Junction on the third pass!

The Digbeth Branch Canal

This was built by 1799 as a short-cut to avoid the 7km 17-lock passage via Salford Junction. A conservation area, it is full of restored features, including the 94m Ashted Tunnel (walk through).

Farmer's Bridge Locks

Or the 'Old Thirteen' on the Birmingham & Fazeley Canal, rise a total of 24.4m (80ft) in the city centre. Here, as the walkway leaflet (see Literature) puts it: 'The canal passes secretly through a canyon of busy city buildings'. Between locks 9 and 10, high-rise buildings have been built right over the canal, which follows its original course. What would the navvies who built it now say to that!

1 *From Aston Junction, go northeast, signed to Salford Junction and continue for 2.5km, as far as the junction beneath Spaghetti Junction.*

2 *At Salford Junction, you need to do a 300° turn clockwise back towards the city, but this isn't immediately evident. From the signpost (follow to Digbeth), turn right staying with the canal on the left and down the left of the ramp to go beneath the bridge (not up the ramp as the sign appears to indicate). Continue for 4km to Bordesley Junction.*

3 *Turn right at the Grand Union Canal, northwest (with the canal on your left – do not cross the black and white bridge). Continue for 800m to Digbeth Junction (Warwick Bar, where the two canals originally separated).*

The best way to view the 1km-long structure that is Spaghetti Junction is from the tranquil parallel world of the waterways below.

4 *At Digbeth Junction go right, signed for Aston Junction on the Digbeth Branch Canal, heading beneath the long Curzon*

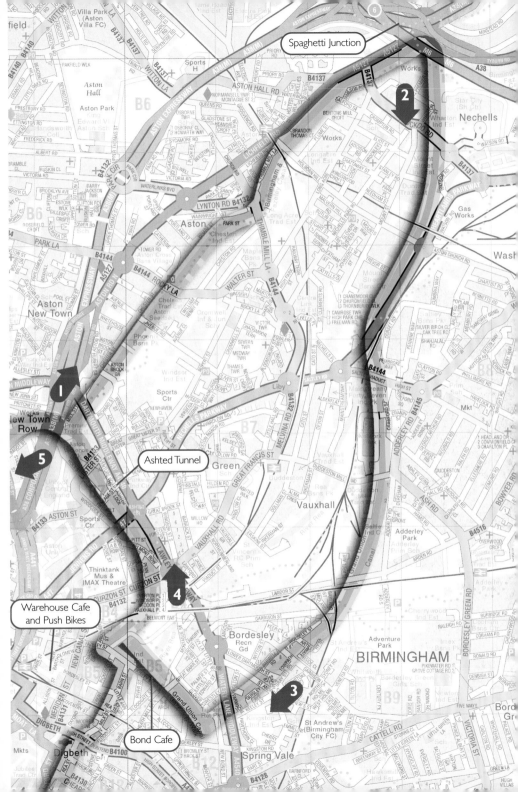

Spaghetti Junction

Nechells

2

Aston New Town

Ashted Tunnel

Green

Vauxhall

1

5

New Town
Row

Warehouse Cafe
and Push Bikes

4

Bordesley

BIRMINGHAM

3

Bond Cafe

Digbeth

Spring Vale

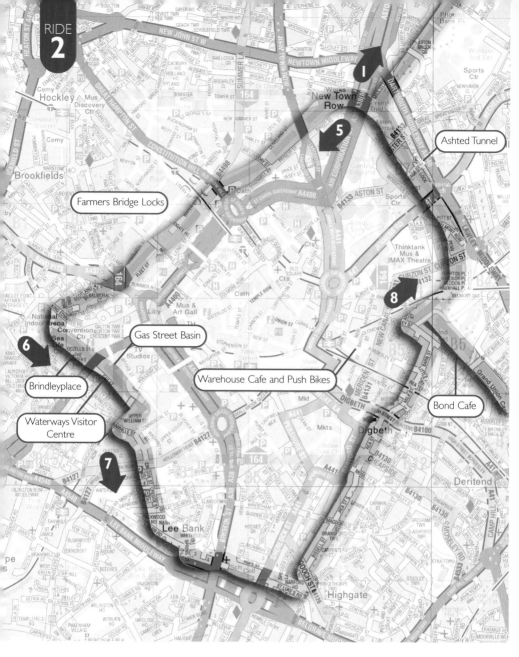

Farmers Bridge Locks

Ashted Tunnel

Gas Street Basin

Brindleyplace

Waterways Visitor Centre

Warehouse Cafe and Push Bikes

Bond Cafe

Street bridge. Continue for 1.5km to Aston Junction. It is compulsory to dismount for the restored flight of six Ashted Locks and the narrow Ashted Tunnel. Modern buildings and year-round planting enhance the section around Aston Science Park – Faraday Wharf at Aston University.

5 *This is the start of the southern city anticlockwise loop; from Aston Junction now turn left, signed for Farmer's Bridge Junction beneath Aston Road Bridge. This again requires compulsory dismounting at locks, low bridges and for blind corners, as the towpath climbs up the 13-strong flight of Farmer's Bridge Locks.*

The turnaround point for the northerly loop – imagine it before the motorway was built!

Continue for 4.5km as far as Old Turn Junction at Brindleyplace, the heart of trendy Birmingham – and the national canal network!

6 Turn left, signed to Worcester, walking across the black and white bridge (beside the Malthouse pub). Proceed carefully, dismount at long Broad Street Bridge and give way to pedestrians throughout. Continue around Gas Street Basin and walk over the ramp back to the straight-through towpath beside the British Waterways visitor centre – pop in for information. This is called Worcester Bar, and is the start of the Worcester & Birmingham Canal.

Stay on the towpath for just 500m, round the right-hand bend (opposite the Mailbox) as far as the first bridge carrying Granville St. Leave the towpath and climb 30 steps.

7 At the road bridge, turn left from the direction you have been travelling (right from the top of the steps). This is the 5km road/paths section. Head along Granville St (bear right soon) and pass the war memorial gardens. After 200m continue straight ahead into Cregoe Street, downhill, and at the end, take the path straight ahead, now on the Central Ring Cycle Route, signed for Highgate (stay with this to Gooch St). Turn left at the bottom on to the road,

with the sign. After 150m, turn right down Spring St and make your way to the traffic lights (Bristol St/Middleway).

Take the subway to the left beneath Bristol St, emerge and continue straight ahead down Hope Street (Matthew Boulton College). At the end, continue straight ahead on the zebra crossing on the pathway to the end, Gooch St.

Dogleg left/right into Bissell St (beside the Sir Charles Napier pub). Continue in the same direction for 1km along Rea St South/Read St to Digbeth High St. Dismount and cross at the pedestrian lights to the right, and remount to continue in the same direction (beside Bull's Head pub) for 500m into Milk St/Barn St (Milk St is one-way, so if travelling in reverse, dismount and walk) to the T-junction with Fazeley St (the building opposite commemorates Fellows, Morton & Clayton, a major canal carrier that had a wharf here). Turn left 200m to see the canal access on the bridge, right.

8 Walk down the brick ramp and at the canalside, turn right on the towpath, back to Warwick Bar/Digbeth Junction. To complete the figure-of-eight, re-ride the Digbeth Branch; continue straight ahead back to Aston Junction (1.5km), again heeding the compulsory dismounts at locks and Ashted Tunnel.

Edgbaston Reservoir, Harborne Walkway and the Two Towers

This pleasant little tour of the reservoir, Main Line Canal and Harborne Walkway rail trail has a healthy low-car content. The Reservoir Cafe beside the entrance is an added bonus.

On the towpath, give way to all other users and follow the Waterways Code, see page 11. The main hazard (apart from a little broken glass on the rail trail and 16 steps up off the towpath) are the roads in the closing

RIDE INFORMATION

Distance	11km (7 miles) including reservoir circuit 3km (2 miles)
Off-road	8km (5 miles) (72%) (5km reservoir, 5km towpath and rail trail)
Grade	Easy

Suitability for children and occasional riders?

The reservoir circuit is excellent (surfaced, car-free and scenic, but ride considerably). Harborne Walkway rail trail (unsurfaced) is good in dry weather. The Main Line Canal towpath is broad and clear and suitable for strong children with good bike control, but the finishing road section is not suitable (see Traffic).

Traffic

1km of roads with quick traffic, although tolerable outside working hours; Harborne Rd/Monument Rd. Use the pedestrian crossing over Hagley Rd.

Start/finish

Edgbaston Reservoir car park at the end of Reservoir Rd.

Stations

Five Ways (1.5km east of Harborne Rd); New Street 1.5km east of St Vincent St (start of towpath).

Refreshments

Reservoir Cafe (Reservoir Rd outside reservoir gateway); Toby Carvery Harborne (Harborne Rd).

Literature

There's a map-leaflet, The Gas Street to Galton Valley Canal Walk, available from British Waterways Gas Street Visitor Centre (Tel: 0121 632 6845).

The Birmingham Canal Navigations map is a good aid to understanding the canals, and shows clearly how the Old and New Main Lines interweave (available from GeoProjects, 9 Southern Court, South St, Reading RG1 4QS, Tel: 0118 939 3567).

The Birmingham Cycling Map (Cycle City Guides, £4.95, from Push Bikes Tel: 0121 632 6753) shows much of the route.

A local lady takes the air at Edgbaston Reservoir.

section. Harborne Road climbs and narrows, with a funny junction at the top, then there's a crossing over Hagley Rd (use the pedestrian lights) into narrow Monument Rd.

What to see
Edgbaston Reservoir
This was built to supply the canals with water and is now a popular place for sailing, boat trips (Mar-Oct) and strolling. Cycling is not officially permitted, but the path is good enough to accommodate bicycles as long as you give way to other users. The Birmingham City Council rangers are on tel: 0121 454 1908.

The Main Line Canal
This 1km section has examples of how the meandering Old Canal (1769) is cut through by the straight New Canal (1838), which we make our route. This is part of the Birmingham to Wolverhampton Main Line Cycleway.

The Harborne Walkway
The Harborne branch railway closed to passengers in 1934 and is now the Harborne Walkway. On the Main Line towpath you can see where the line came off the main railway over the brick pier in the middle of the canal. The last part down to Chad Valley follows a notably high bosky embankment. The walkway is unsurfaced and only easy to ride in dry weather. To ride it in wet weather you need grippy tyres

and a tolerance of wet feet. Watch for broken glass in a few places beneath the bridges.

The Two Towers, Waterworks Rd
This pair is thought to have been an inspiration for JRR Tolkein's *The Two Towers*. Perrott's Folly

The Two Towers.

Edgbaston Reservoir is a great open space in the centre, with good views of the city.

was built in 1758 by John Perrott so that he could look over his land, and has been used as an observatory. The ornate Victorian tower at the waterworks is actually a boilerhouse chimney.

Peace Pagoda

On Osler St (right before the reservoir gateway) is the Dhamma-Talaka Peace Pagoda, a buddhist temple.

1 Start at the car park at Edgbaston Reservoir, accessed from Reservoir Rd on the southeastern flank. Before setting out for the 'outside' tour you can ride a circuit (3km) of the reservoir. Please give way to all other users.

Head away from the reservoir along Reservoir Road, then dogleg carefully over Monument Rd at the end into little Ladywood Rd. After 150m, turn left into Holy Well Close, and take the subway at the end, beneath the Middleway dual carriageway. At the far side, continue in the same direction into St Vincent St West, going straight ahead on the pathway, crossing Great Tindal St to the canal bridge.

2 Access the Main Line Canal on the near side of the bridge and turn left (from the direction of travel) northwest (with the canal on

your right); the cycleway actually uses the right bank towpath). Continue straight ahead for 1km, passing Rotton Park Junction after 800m, as far as the brick pier in the centre of the canal.

3 Leave the towpath left, climb the path up the steep bank (16 steps at the top). At the top, in Northbrook Rd, look across and right (Coplow St) and take the pathway on the green space between the houses – this is the course of the old railway.

Continue over Barford Rd (beside the school) and bear right on the track beneath the bridge. Emerge the other side in Summerfield Park and continue for 1km in the same direction through the park (ignore numerous crosspaths). Just before the end (Rotton Park Rd), alongside the line of poplars, turn left down the bank to pick up the line of the rail trail below, and continue in the same direction beneath the bridge.

4 Now on Harborne Walk, continue for 2km but after 1km, stay on the high embankment. At the end, stay with the path to exit between housing at Forest Drive. Turn right into Park Hill Rd and then immediately right again into Moor Pool Ave (to corkscrew beneath the bridge you have just crossed).

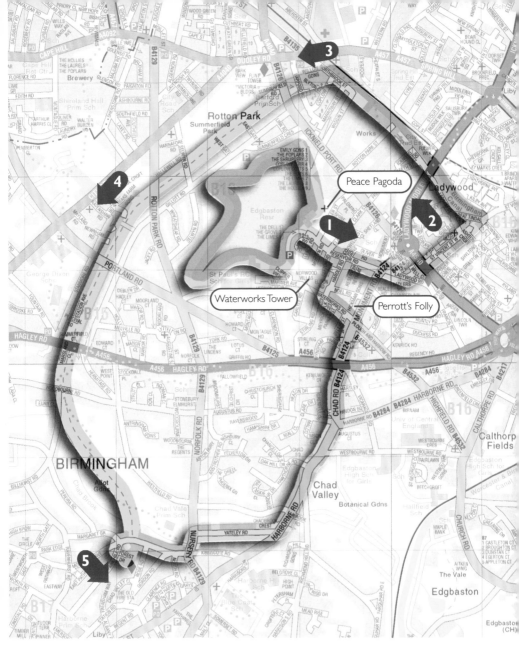

5 It is now roads all the way back to the reservoir. Continue to the end of Nursery Rd, dogleg left/right into Yateley Rd and carry on to the end to turn left into Harborne Rd. Climb, and watch the traffic as the road narrows. Watch also the junction at the top (with Augustus Rd), and continue (now on Chad Rd) to the big junction with Hagley Rd.

Cross (there are pedestrian lights) and continue straight ahead into Monument Rd, another relatively tight one. After 400m turn left into Waterworks Rd beside Perrott's Folly. The waterworks tower lies 100m further past Harold Rd, where we go right back to Reservoir Rd.

North Birmingham green circuit,

via Sutton Park and Spaghetti Junction

It's water, water much of the way, through parks, heathland and towpaths to beneath the motorway morass that somehow works so well.

This official cycle route follows a pleasingly green circuit round the suburbs north of the M6. Head out on pleasant parkland paths, traverse the glorious heathland of Sutton Park, return south via new Newhall Country Park and close the circle on the Birmingham & Fazeley and Tame Valley canals.

As yet, one section in the east is incomplete, along Plants Brook south of Newhall Country Park. For the time being, while negotiations are on-going, you have to divert along roads for 3km. The hope is one day to continue on an upgraded brookside path to Pype Hayes Park. Also, the route was ridden before all the signs had gone in, so forgive us if reality varies slightly from our description.

Sutton Park, at the north end of the route, is lovely and calming. At the southern end of the route, the legs of Spaghetti Junction are a spectacle. Having predated elevated motorways by 200 years, the waterways provide a peaceful through-route at ground level while traffic rips about overhead. The towpaths beneath the 1km web of flyovers

RIDE INFORMATION

Distance	20km (13 miles)
Car-free	14.5km (9 miles) (72%)
Grade	Moderate (there are some rises, and it's not a shortie)

Suitability for children and occasional riders?

The circuit is currently broken at Plants Brook, requiring a 3km diversion on very busy roads, which makes the tour as a whole bad for children. However, you can just explore Sutton Park or Brookvale Park. Children need to have good handling to ride on towpaths, although these sections are in particularly good condition.

Traffic

The road section through Sutton Coldfield in the north, between Sutton Park and Newhall Country Park, is low-traffic with assisted crossings. But, the diversion around the incomplete section of off-road route, down the eastern side between Newhall Country Park and Pype Hayes Park, is on very busy roads.

Start/finish

There are three possibilities (in addition to starting anywhere en route); at Brookvale Park (Park Road, Stockland Green, our starting point – a car park but no cafe); at two points in Sutton Park (en route at Banner's Gate where there's a car park but no cafe; at the main Sutton Coldfield entrance, (see Sutton Park route page 38, car parks, cafe and

Deykin Avenue Lock, the final one of the route, just beyond Spaghetti Junction.

are clear and repaved, so there's nothing creepy about them. Separately, at two points the canal runs beneath long warehouses, but again the path is clear and broad, so there's nothing to worry about.

On the towpath, give way to other users and observe the Waterways Code see page 11. Note that the anti-motorbike barriers on the towpaths are awkward at the best of times, and very hard to negotiate with trailerbikes, panniers or recumbents. These barriers occur intermittently.

visitor centre); at Pype Hayes Hall, Pype Hayes Park, off the A452 Chester Rd (car park, no cafe).

Stations
Aston (1km south), Gravelly Hill (800m east).

Refreshments
Cafe in Sutton Park (500m off route, continue at the 5-way junction where the directions go right).

Literature
The Birmingham Canal Navigations map is a good aid to understanding the canals (available from GeoProjects, 9 Southern Court, South St, Reading RG1 4QS).

Singing in the rain perhaps, at Witton Lakes.

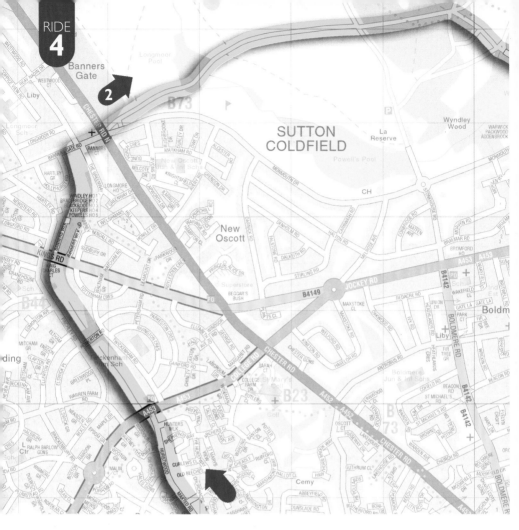

1 (See map on p.36) From the southern end of Brookvale Park (off Park Rd), head along the left bank of the lake to the end. Cross right, over George Rd, and continue in the same direction along short Boulton Walk. At the end, cross over Marsh Hill and take the parkland track, Riverside Path, in the same direction (with the stream on your left). Soon, you reach Witton Lakes; ride up beside the dam, follow the path along the right bank and continue on the tarmac path to the end (Perry Common Rd).

Cross over and continue in the same direction for 2.5km on brookside cycle paths, crossing three roads. At the B4149 dual carriageway (by Roger Slater, butchers) cross straight over, and go up, over and down the open space (no path).

At Banner's Gate Road at the bottom (beside The Greenway), turn right towards the traffic lights (A452, Chester Rd), then straight over again, and enter Sutton Park by Banner's Gate on the left.

2 In Sutton Park, continue in the same direction for 2km, passing Longmoor Pool on the left and then go straight over at a tarmac crossroads (watch for a small amount of park traffic). From there, the roadway dips downhill, and after 500m, before reaching the bottom, fork right at what is actually a five-way tarmac junction. (For the cafe and visitor centre continue for 500m).

Continue to the river ford, cross, pass through

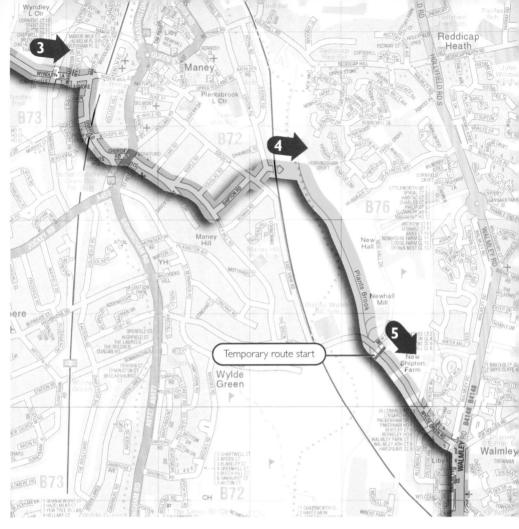

the barrier and continue past Wyndley Pool Lake on your right to reach the perimeter of Sutton Park at Somerville Rd.

3 Cross over carefully and continue in the same direction up the steep roadway (Wyndley Lane).

At the top (Manor Hill), go right carefully (Driffold), for 500m then, 150m before the main road at the bottom, fork left along Church Rd. At the bottom, cross over Birmingham Rd (A5127) and continue in the same direction up Maney Hill Rd for 800m. Take the fourth left, Shipton Rd, to the bottom and make a dogleg right/left into Ebrook Rd. After 100m go off the road beneath the railway arch and into Newhall Country Park.

4 On the far side of the arch, take the leftmost of three tracks, at 10 o'clock from the concrete disc, and head for Plants Brook. Cross the bridge and turn right along the left bank of the stream and continue for 1.6km to Wylde Green Road.

5 (This is where we have to divert on to busy roads and dual carriageways for 3km while negotiations for a track along Plants Brook to Pype Hayes Park continue.)

Turn left up the hill and follow the road to the crossroads with Walmley Rd. Turn right carefully into Walmley Rd which becomes Eachelhurst Rd. After 2.5km continue straight over at the roundabout with Chester Rd.

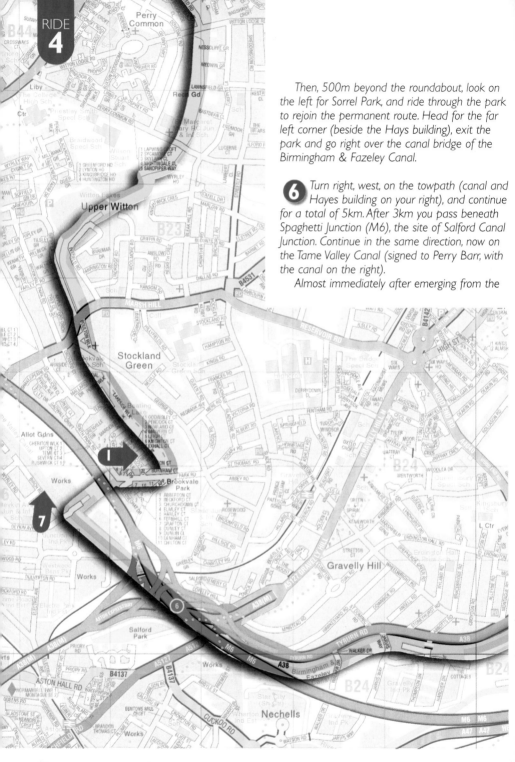

Then, 500m beyond the roundabout, look on the left for Sorrel Park, and ride through the park to rejoin the permanent route. Head for the far left corner (beside the Hays building), exit the park and go right over the canal bridge of the Birmingham & Fazeley Canal.

6 Turn right, west, on the towpath (canal and Hayes building on your right), and continue for a total of 5km. After 3km you pass beneath Spaghetti Junction (M6), the site of Salford Canal Junction. Continue in the same direction, now on the Tame Valley Canal (signed to Perry Barr, with the canal on the right).

Almost immediately after emerging from the

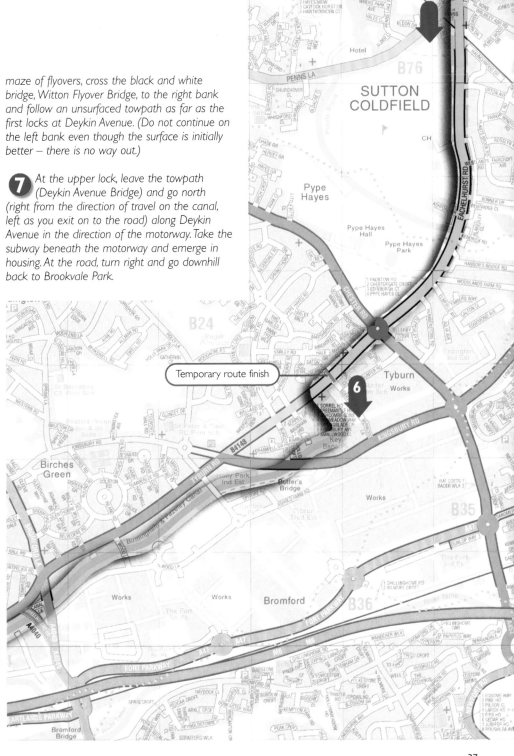

maze of flyovers, cross the black and white
bridge, Witton Flyover Bridge, to the right bank
and follow an unsurfaced towpath as far as the
first locks at Deykin Avenue. (Do not continue on
the left bank even though the surface is initially
better – there is no way out.)

7 At the upper lock, leave the towpath
(Deykin Avenue Bridge) and go north
(right from the direction of travel on the canal,
left as you exit on to the road) along Deykin
Avenue in the direction of the motorway. Take the
subway beneath the motorway and emerge in
housing. At the road, turn right and go downhill
back to Brookvale Park.

Temporary route finish

Sutton Park Scamper

A mountain bike tour of a medieval hunting park where Exmoor ponies now graze

Sutton Park is a natural treasure. This large pocket of heath and woodland has been managed and preserved for over 1,000 years, and in 1997, became a National Nature Reserve. The park is home to a rich variety of flora and fauna, including lizards, the rare water shrew and unique species of spider. In late summer, gorse and heather colour the landscape while a glossy herd of Exmoor ponies grazes the northern woods.

There are seven lovely lakes including the atmospheric Bracebridge Pool which is passed en route.

Designated a deer park in 1126, as much to provide venison for the table as for sport, the park also features archaeological remains from much older times. 'Burnt mounds', Bronze Age cooking sites, exist at the northern tip, and a straight, 2.5km stretch of the Roman Ryknild Street runs along the western edge. This connected forts at Wall near Lichfield and Metchley in Edgbaston.

RIDE INFORMATION

Distance	11km (7 miles)
Off-road	10km (6 miles) (1.5km of park roadway) (91%)
Grade	Moderate off-road

Suitability for children and occasional riders?
The full mountain bike circuit is good for older, stronger children. A short circuit on the park roads (which carry very little traffic) suits little ones. The full circuit is ideal for starter mountain bikers, and pootling around the estate roads is good for all ages.

Traffic
Nominal

Start/finish
Sutton Park Visitor Centre (tel: 0121 355 6370), near the main Town Gate entrance, 500m northwest of Sutton Coldfield centre (6.5km north M6, J5). There is also parking at points on the route: Banners Gate (1.6km round) and the Boathouse Restaurant (5km round).

Stations
Sutton Coldfield (500m east).

Refreshments
Cafes at Town Gate (open daily all-year round) and as part of the Boathouse Restaurant at Bracebridge Pool (also, off the main route at Powell's Pool).

What to see
Exmoor ponies in the northern part; displays telling Sutton Park's story at the visitor centre; model aircraft flying.

Literature
Sutton Park - National Nature Reserve explains the park's history and details some sites. A rather old-fashioned and not terribly accurate map is also available. Both are free from the visitor centre.

Sutton Park is also a pleasant place to cycle, with refreshments never far away. A good six kilometres of car-free roadway makes an excellent surface for easy pedallers and little children (and mostly branches out from the visitor centre). For mountain bikers there are enough designated trails – you are not permitted to ride freely – to last an hour or so: longer if you get lost. This route, through undulating, changing landscape is quite easy, and has a handful of sub-minute climbs. The steepest is up Rowton Bank, and there's one short, rooty bank with steps beyond the turn for the Boathouse Restaurant in the last quarter of the ride.

The route starts from the visitor centre and runs first through sandy open southern heathland, then the wooded northern area. Up there, around Bracebridge Pool, it's easy to get lost, but most tracks lead to the same place in the end. Watch for walkers, and for ponies in the northern part. In the woods the paths get very muddy after rain, while in the southern heathland, the soil drains well.

The route soon passes Longmoor Pool.

Left: The totem pole near the North Gate.
Above: Lovely, leafy riding in what is a National Nature Reserve.

1 Start from the visitor centre, 300m inside from the main entrance at Town Gate. From there, head 200m back to the six-way roadway junction. Take the second exit (surfaced, with grass on the left, woodland on the right). Continue in the same direction for 2.4km through the plantation, straight ahead at the crossroads, past the model aircraft flying area (on the right), and down past Longmoor Pool to Banners Gate car park.

2 Turn right and head out of the corner of the car park, past the toilets (at an acute angle, 4 o'clock to your arrival) then on a clear off-road track. Continue in the same direction for 1km, across grassland followed by woods and then open heathland, to a clear cross-tracks with a better gravelled track which is very straight. Turn right (towards the pine clump) and continue in the same direction for 1km, climbing sharply up Rowton Bank to the roadway (the Jamboree Memorial Stone).

3 Go left on the road and shortly, after 500m (the golf course on the left), turn right at a gorse hedgerow at right-angles to the roadway. Ride beside the hedgerow on a lightly marked grass track, to where it meets the plantation. Where the vegetation closes in (and overhead) turn left on a clear grass track across the open grassy arena field. Continue to the pebbled standing, beside the trees. Head right into the trees on the wide track, continue over the railway line and down through woods to Bracebridge Pool. This is Exmoor pony land.

4 After Bracebridge Pool things become a little muddled on a bracken-covered hillside riven with tracks. But, if you miss the track, they all more or less come out at the top of the hill at the correct main track which goes off to the right.

With the pool on the right-hand side, keep going in the same direction for 100m (ignore tracks forking off right) to a fork with a tree and seat in the middle. Take the right fork here, and climb stiffly for 50m to a five-way track junction at a plantation. Turn left, away from the woodland, go uphill along a narrower track for 200m. At a T-junction with a broad gravel track, turn right. This closes down to a 4WD track in trees, going downhill to a tarmac road and parking.

The Boathouse Restaurant and tea kiosk on the lakeside is 100m to the right.

5 Cross straight over the road and on to another track towards trees. After 100m, head leftwards and take care down a steep rooted track with steps. At the bottom, find a gate in the wire fence leading to a track which crosses the railway embankment. Beyond the railway line, turn left along the unsurfaced track, with Blackroot Pool on your right. Emerge at a car park and turn slightly right to continue on grass for 500m, sloping gently downhill. At the bottom, at the roadway, turn left and back to the main entrance and refreshment kiosk near the visitor centre.

A herd of Exmoor ponies (a little far from home) grazes freely in the northern part of the park.

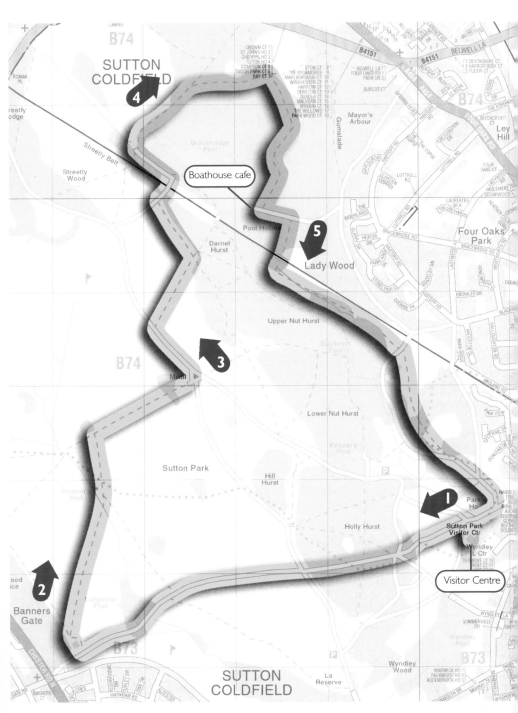

East Birmingham green circuit, via the airport

Enjoy 20km of car-free waterside riding round the River Cole and Grand Union Canal – with some planespotting in Sheldon Country Park.

Cars hardly count on this suburban green circuit as you track the River Cole its little tributaries and the Grand Union Canal, in one big circle. The route explores a virtually unbroken line of waterside paths for 19km, with just a 3km link on the road between brook and canal.

The highlight is snicking the end of Birmingham International Airport runway in Sheldon Country Park, where flights pass close overhead on take-off and landing. Children will also like the pigs, chickens and the prize-winning herd of Jersey cows munching at Old Rectory Farm nearby.

On the towpath, please give way to other users and observe the Waterways Code, see page 11. Note that the anti-motorbike

RIDE INFORMATION

Distance   22.5km (14 miles)
Car-free   19km (12 miles) (86%)

Grade
Easy with very little road riding; this follows mostly flat parkland tracks, some surfaced, with a handful of short rough sections that mean the complete circuit is best ridden on a mountain bike – especially after wet weather.

Suitability for children and occasional riders?
There's plenty of car-free riding here, and, in good weather, certain surfaced sections of parkland track (see below) are ideal. However, only children with good bike control should ride the 3km towpath section. An improving rider could tackle the circuit as a whole – it's 95 per cent flat and straightforward handling-wise.

Traffic
Only on road crossings and the road link from Coventry Rd in Sheldon to the Grand Union Canal in Olton.

Start/finish
Small Heath/Heybarnes Circus (park in side roads off Heybarnes Rd), also in Sheldon Country Park near Old Rectory Farm.

Stations
Stechford, Marston Green, Olton, Acock's Green, Tyseley.

Refreshments
Cafe at Asda Small Heath; cafe at Old Rectory Farm.

What to see
Planespotting at Birmingham International Airport; the animals at Old Rectory Farm in Sheldon Country Park.

Mown meadows alongside the River Cole.   Below: A bit of countryside in the urban sprawl.

barriers on the towpaths are awkward at the best of times, and very hard to negotiate with trailerbikes, panniers or recumbents. These occur intermittently.

For the sake of pinpointing a start point, we choose the Heybarnes Circus roundabout near Asda at Small Heath on the River Cole, but a good alternative is near Old Rectory Farm itself in Sheldon Country Park, where there is a car park and you could run anticlockwise to avoid an initial road section.

Being only part-surfaced, this ride is best in dry weather on a mountain bike. After rain, you have to love mud to enjoy yourself. The route's northerly arc follows the Cole through a mix of scenic and plain parkland. The eastern flank beside Kingshurst Brook is very well groomed, and followed by a track through the grassland of Sheldon Country Park. The Grand Union Canal towpath starts leafy and turns industrial.

Some park and woodland sections are lonely, and in a handful of places the track remains rideable but turns narrow and rough for a short distance, ie beneath the railway bridges at Stechford and at Marston Green. You must duck low beneath the road bridge

at Cole Hall Lane in Buckland End. There are steps down to join the canal towpath from the road in Olton.

Good sections for young children include the surfaced parkland track between Small Heath and Stechford (3km), and the run between Babb's Mill, Kingshurst and Chelmsley Wood – the cycle paths beside Kingshurst Brook are perfection (3km). Old Rectory Farm in Sheldon Country Park is also a good starting/finishing point for a 3km round trip (on dirt track only) between the farm animals and the airport runway.

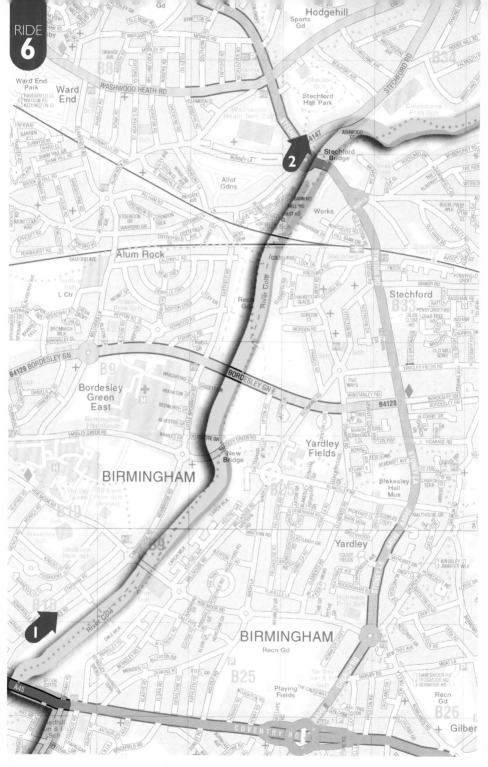

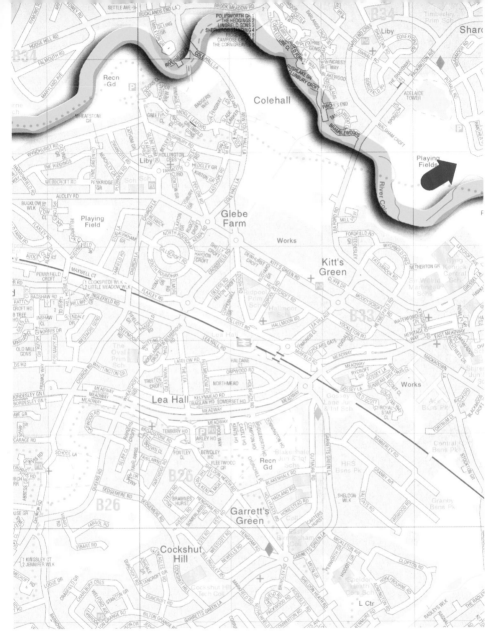

1 *Start from the east side of Heybarnes Circus and follow the parkland riverside track northwards through Hay Barn Recreation Ground. Continue on well-surfaced bankside tracks beside the river for 3km as far as the main Stechford Lane (crossing three roads en route, and passing on rough singletrack beneath the railway line).*

2 *Cross over Stechford Lane and continue in the same direction on the dirt track to the left of Stechford bridge and along this winding, occasionally narrow and rough wood and grassland track for 5.5km (after 2.5km duck low beneath the road bridge, Cole Hall Lane) to Babb's Mill, which is beside a cycling fingerpost before a lake.*

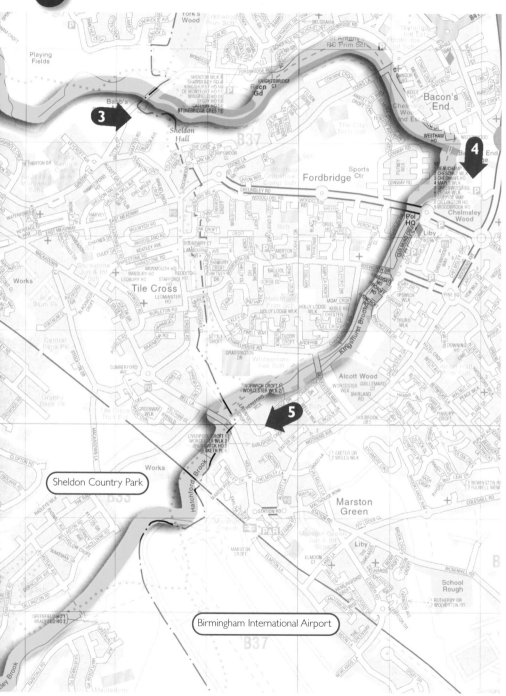

'Not a very pretty model, I'm afraid', said this chap as he rode past on the Grand Union Canal.

3 Continue for 1.5km in the same direction, signed to Chelmsley Wood, with the lake on the left (there are paths on both sides of the river, the southerly farside track is official and better-surfaced). At the next road, (Cook's Lane, Ford Bridge/Kingshurst), cross over and take either the left or right bank paths to the river footbridge beside the landscaped playground (Bacon's End).

4 This is the point where the route turns south to follow Kingshurst Brook. At the footbridge, go right 'to Alcott Wood and Sheldon' on dreamy-smooth cycle paths on the west bank of the river. At the first road (Chelmsley Rd) cross to the leftside east bank, and continue beside the stream for another 1.5km (crossing Bosworth Drive and the river on a footbridge 300m after the second road crossing, Gloucester Way).

5 At the end of the parkland, cross Holly Lane and enter Sheldon Country Park on

a narrow dirt track with a brook to the left. After 300m, pass beneath the railway arches (rough but rideable) and fork right on the track to reach the airport runway viewpoint. Continue in the same direction for another 1.5km on rough but rideable tracks (dry weather permitting), then follow Westley Brook over trackless King George V Memorial playing fields. Exit the fields via the roadway on the right (leading to the country park car park). Old Rectory Farm is on the left. Leave the open space on the tarmac roadway (Ragley Drive) to the T-junction with Church Lane. Turn left. After 200m, turn right through the last part of Sheldon Country Park, still tracking the brook. Continue in the same direction (no need to cross to the other bank) for 1km to the dual carriageway (Coventry Rd A45).

6 Cross using the subway to the left, and take Lyndon Rd (beside Safeway),

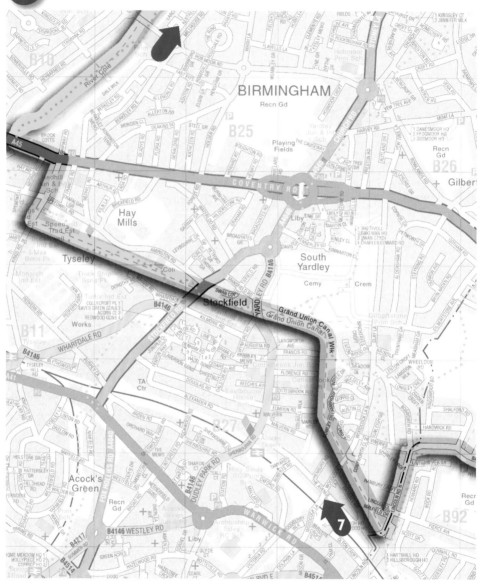

continuing in the same direction. Follow this for 800m, then turn right into Barn Lane. Continue for 800m to the crossroads with Lincoln Rd North, and turn left. After 500m, the road rises over the Grand Union Canal. Take the steps down, right, off the bridge to the towpath.

7 Turn right, north, along the canal and continue for 3km to exit up the clear paved ramp beside the road bridge at Kings Rd. Turn right, north, on Kings Rd, continue for 400m to the dual carriageway (Coventry Rd A45 again), then left for 400m and back to Heybarnes Circus.

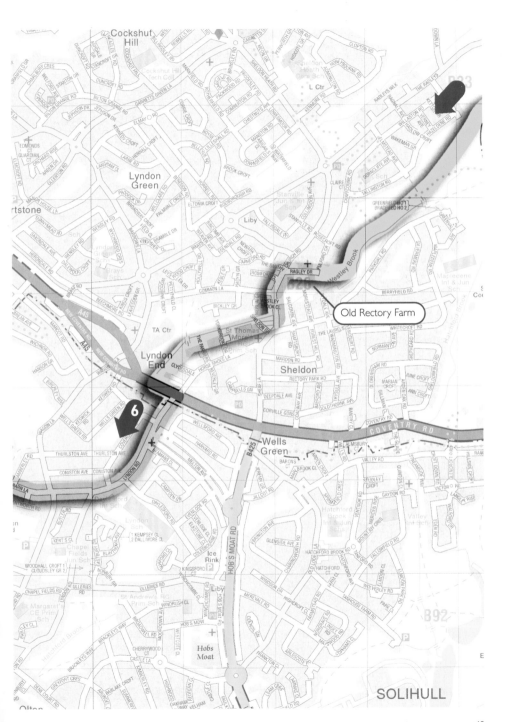

Old Rectory Farm

SOLIHULL

South Birmingham green circuit

A winning parkland and towpath tour that swings between the city centre and surburbia, via the River Rea, Grand Union Canal, River Cole and Stratford upon Avon Canal.

How many inhabitants of south Brum know how good their local car-free cycling is – with good places to eat too?

This is a good-length leafy waterside circuit you can pick up at any point between Digbeth and King's Norton, and ride back to where you started via a dozen pleasant places, with hardly an exhaust for company. The route is obvious and rideable throughout, and good-looking in most parts. Even the road-link through Digbeth from the River Rea to the Grand Union Canal is relatively painless.

Landscaping has enhanced the transition between the Grand Union Canal and River Cole path at the Ackers (Small Heath), beside the climbing walls of the adventure centre. From there the Cole runs south through parkland for 5km, through Sparkhill and

RIDE INFORMATION

Distance	22km (14 miles)
Car-free	19km (12 miles) (86%)
Grade	Easy-moderate

Suitable for children and occasional riders?
Cannon Hill Park is ideal for little children, as well as the southerly continuation of the River Rea cycle route. As a whole, the route can be completed by strong, experienced children – assuming their bike control is good enough for towpaths (3km on the Grand Union at the city centre end, 5km on the Stratford upon Avon Canal at the southern end). The terrain is flat, but down the River Cole and along Chinn Brook you find yourself pushing over trackless grass.

Traffic
Several road crossings present little problem. The first kilometre of the road section towards the city centre is on a quiet, signposted cycle route. The second kilometre is through an industrial area, busy on weekdays with occasional heavy lorries and buses.

Start/finish
On the western, extra-child-friendly flank, start at the car park at Cannon Hill Park either near the Midlands Arts Centre (MAC) off Edgbaston Rd, or at the southern end near the Nature Centre off Pershore Rd. On the eastern flank of the route, Sarehole Mill has a car park (there is also casual car parking outside Drucker's Vienna Patisserie on Stratford Rd on route).

Stations
Bordesley, Small Heath, Tyseley, Hall Green, Yardley Wood, King's Norton, Bournville.

Refreshments
There are some very good options. Cafes in Cannon Hill Park at the MAC and the Park Tearoom; the Warehouse Cafe (Tel: 0121 633 0261, 54 Allison St, in the same building

One of the bonuses of living in Birmingham:
Cannon Hill Park.

as Push Bikes and the Cycle Chain bike shop)
lies 400m off-route in Digbeth – go left off
Milk St up Bordesley St; the Bond cafe on
Fazeley St, Digbeth, backing on to the Grand
Union Canal; Druckers Vienna Patisserie
(open 9.30am-5pm Mon-Sat) at the Stratford
Rd crossing on the River Cole.

What to see
Sarehole Mill (Tolkein's inspiration, open
1pm-4pm Tues-Fri, noon-4pm Sat-Sun Easter-
Oct, Tel: 0121-777 6612); Moseley Bog (more
background to *Lord of the Rings*, Yardley Wood
Rd); the Central Mosque (1980).

Literature
The Birmingham Canal Navigations map is a
good aid to understanding the canals
(available from GeoProjects, 9 Southern
Court, South St, Reading RG1 4QS, Tel: 0118
939 3567). The West Midlands Cycle Route
(NCN5) map is available from Sustrans
(Tel: 0117 929 0888) and shows the full linear
route in detail.

Springfield, past Sarehole Mill (in the district
where JRR Tolkein grew up and which
provided inspiration for Middle Earth) down
to Yardley Wood. Turn westward at Chinn
Brook, across a long kilometre of trackless
grassland, then follow 5km of picturesque and
interesting towpath on the Stratford upon
Avon Canal. At the tranquil junction with the
Worcester & Birmingham Canal at King's
Norton you can pause briefly on benches
before turning north on the signposted,
surfaced West Midlands cycle route (NCN5).
After just 1km in Stirchley this turns on to
the River Rea and heads north through well-
tended parkland for 5km, to the end of
much-loved Cannon Hill Park (site of the
Midlands Arts Centre with cafe, galleries,
cinema, bookshops). Thereafter, on streets
near the the city centre, follow NCN5 and
straightforward backroads to the Grand
Union Canal – watch out for lorries on
working days.

On the towpaths, give way to other users
and observe the Waterways Code, see page
11. Take care on slippery towpaths and
approaches, and mind your head on several
low bridges. At the Ackers there are 23 steps
to climb from the canal to the cycle path.

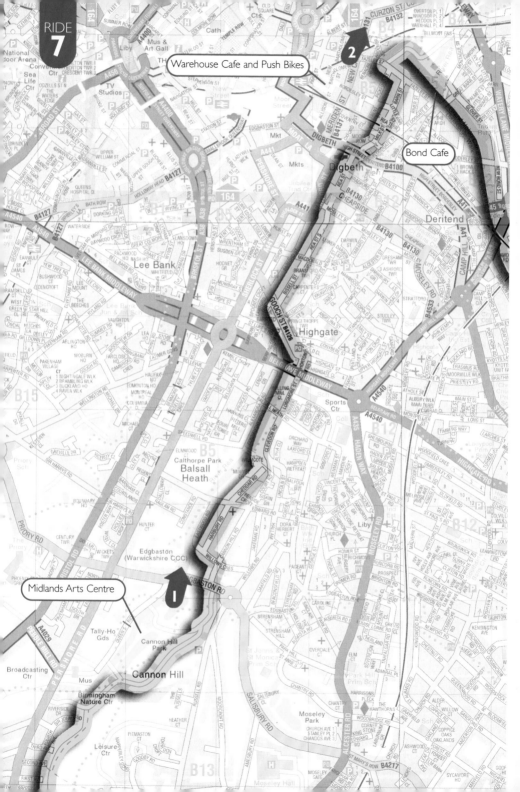

Warehouse Cafe and Push Bikes

Bond Cafe

Midlands Arts Centre

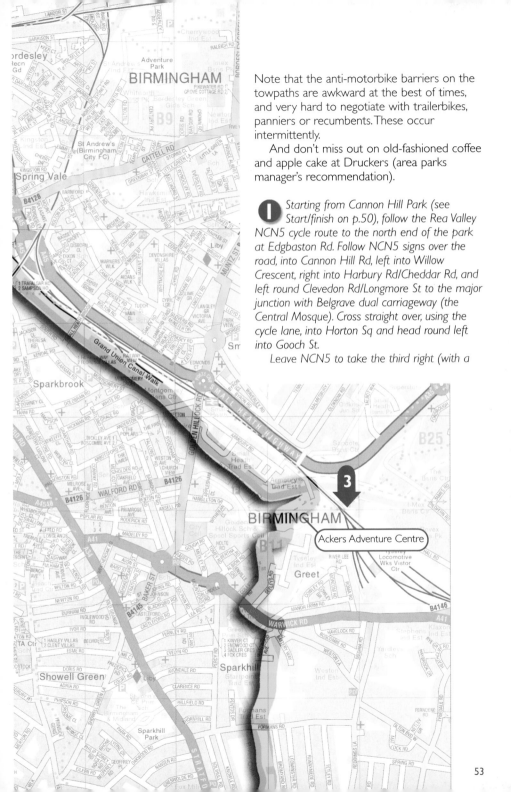

Note that the anti-motorbike barriers on the towpaths are awkward at the best of times, and very hard to negotiate with trailerbikes, panniers or recumbents. These occur intermittently.

And don't miss out on old-fashioned coffee and apple cake at Druckers (area parks manager's recommendation).

1 *Starting from Cannon Hill Park (see Start/finish on p.50), follow the Rea Valley NCN5 cycle route to the north end of the park at Edgbaston Rd. Follow NCN5 signs over the road, into Cannon Hill Rd, left into Willow Crescent, right into Harbury Rd/Cheddar Rd, and left round Clevedon Rd/Longmore St to the major junction with Belgrave dual carriageway (the Central Mosque). Cross straight over, using the cycle lane, into Horton Sq and head round left into Gooch St.*

Leave NCN5 to take the third right (with a

Ackers Adventure Centre

pub on the corner) into Bissell St. Continue straight ahead into Rea St and on to the end at High St. Cross at the pedestrian crossing, and stay in the same direction along Milk St/Barn St to the T-junction with Fazeley St. Turn left, and after 200m, the canal access will be seen on the right.

2 Walk down to the towpath (slippery in the wet), turn right, go over the bridge and turn right again along the Grand Union Canal (Warwick Bar). Pass the Bond on the right (a cafe nestles here amid residential narrowboat moorings beside a converted warehouse). Continue on the same canal for 3km, past Bordesley Junction and Camp Hill Locks (6). At the black and white iron bridge, leave the canal and climb a flight of steps and cross over.

3 Take the driveway straight ahead through the trees, and down to the Ackers adventure centre. Turn left round the clubhouse, cross the wooden bridge and stay on that track past the climbing walls. Continue for 500m on the Project Kingfisher cycle path (go right at the fork after the bridge), and emerge, via a short street, at the main road (Warwick Rd).

Follow the cycle signs to cross first the cycle lights (main Warwick Rd) then the zebra (Weston Lane). Head into the modern industrial estate and take the off-road track on the right. (Beyond the barrier, straight ahead is more direct, as right goes beside the River Cole.) Continue in this direction through River Cole parkland for 5km to Yardley Wood, crossing minor roads and some trackless grassland, switching banks when necessary.

En route after 800m, pass Druckers Vienna Patisserie (open 9.30am-5pm Mon-Sat); after 1.5km comes the ford at Green Rd and after 2km, comes Sarehole Mill Museum. For Moseley Bog, 500m off route from Sarehole Mill, turn right at Cole Bank Road past the mill, right at the roundabout (Wake Green Rd), first left into Thirlmere Drive and then second right into Pensby Close.

Sarehole Mill is now a little museum and visitor centre.

Emerging at an open road junction, cross straight over the road (Trittiford Rd) towards the open space ahead in Chinn Brook Recreation Ground (leave the River Cole as it turns left through Trittiford Mill Park). Take the road in the same direction on the right (Chinn Brook Rd) and after 250m, turn left down the track that leads to the brook, then turn right along the grass track this side of the brook. Continue for 1km. At Yardley Wood Road (Firth Drive) turn left uphill and at the canal bridge at the top, join the canal on the right, going carefully down a steep slipway.

4 Follow the pretty Stratford upon Avon Canal west for 5km. After 2.5km, there is a short tunnel without a towpath. To go over the top and rejoin the canal, continue on the path above it, emerge at a road junction (Monyhull Rd), go over in the same direction, down the grass and into the first left (Shelfield Rd) to regain the towpath via the access point on the

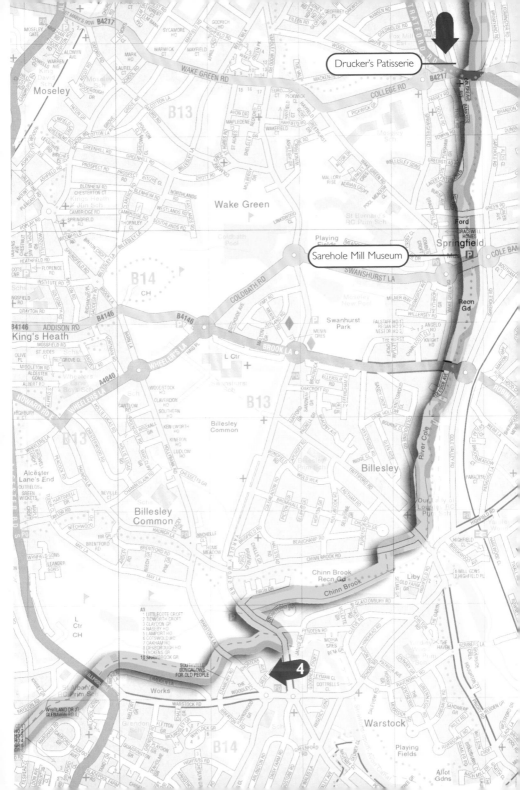

Drucker's Patisserie

Sarehole Mill Museum

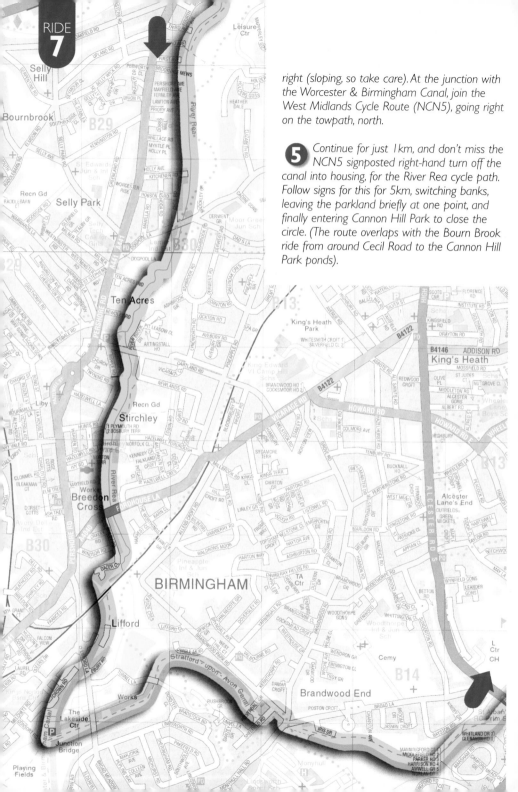

right (sloping, so take care). At the junction with the Worcester & Birmingham Canal, join the West Midlands Cycle Route (NCN5), going right on the towpath, north.

5 Continue for just 1km, and don't miss the NCN5 signposted right-hand turn off the canal into housing, for the River Rea cycle path. Follow signs for this for 5km, switching banks, leaving the parkland briefly at one point, and finally entering Cannon Hill Park to close the circle. (The route overlaps with the Bourn Brook ride from around Cecil Road to the Cannon Hill Park ponds).

Pedestrians and cyclists don't get their feet wet at Sarehole Ford, but cars go the old-fashioned way.

Below: The picturesque junction of the Stratford on Avon canal and Worcester and Birmingham canal in King's Norton.

Country Lanes
from Earlswood to Forhill
back via Hollywood

A road ride that straddles the rural Worcestershire/Warwickshire border south of Birmingham – with a good selection of pubs.

Twelve kilometres south of central Birmingham you find yourself in the Worcestershire and Warwickshire countryside without even crossing the M42.

This straightforward road ride is suitable for all types of bike and cyclist, especially those seeking a liquid lunch on a sunny Sunday. The characterful pubs all have gardens – the Blue Bell at Waring's Green is canalside, while the menus at the Peacock and the Coach & Horses mean you have to book for Sunday lunch. Picturesque features include Earlswood Lakes, popular with anglers and sailors; a challenging climb at Forhill; and pleasant stretch of rural canal towpath (which gets puddly in wet weather) between Dicken's Heath new village and Waring's Green.

This route is typical of dozens of green circuits on the city's limits. Arm yourself with the Ordance Survey map (Landranger 31) and help yourself to the rest. On the canal, please give way to other users and follow the Waterways Code, see page 11.

The Earlswood Craft Centre start/finish

RIDE INFORMATION

Distance	22.5km (14 miles)
Car-free	5km (3 miles) on the Stratford upon Avon Canal (22%)
Grade	Easy-moderate

Suitability for children and occasional riders?
So-so. There's one big hill on the lane up to Forhill (which you can nevertheless by-pass), and fast passing traffic in the latter half.

Traffic
This is fast in places: in the second half between Forhill and Hollywood, and around Whitlock End.

Start/finish
Start anywhere on the circuit. We've chosen Earlswood Craft Centre for the sake of the cafe and parking.

Stations
Earlswood, Whitlock's End.

Refreshments
Poppy's Tearoom & Restaurant at Earlswood Craft Centre; the Coach & Horses pub in Weatheroak Hill; the Peacock pub at Forhill; the Blue Bell beside the canal at Waring's Green.

What to see
Rural scenery; craft workshops at Earlswood Craft Centre (a converted redbrick farm).

The ride starts at Earlswood Craft Centre, where there's an attractive cafe.

point is a feature in itself. The handsome redbrick farm has been converted into workshops and a cafe with lots of space where cyclists are welcome.

Some traffic notes. Crossing the A435 dual carriageway in each direction cyclists are segregated from the cars, but you must expect fast-moving vehicles in the second-half from Forhill via Hollywood through Whitlock's End to the towpath. Splash or cross the ford of the River Cole (which we ride in length on the South Brum green circular) near Trueman's Heath.

Beyond Whitlock's End, the new housing and road layout at Dickens Heath village is not shown on the map, so follow the route directions carefully.

1 *(See p.62) Coming out of Earlswood Craft Centre, turn right, west (Wood Lane) and continue for 1km to a T-junction. Turn left, signed to Earlswood station. After 1km on the far side of Earlswood station, turn right signed to Tanners Green. At that hamlet, take the second left, Barkers Lane. Continue to the dual-carriageway A435.*

2 *(See p.60) Turn left, south (on the pavement if you prefer) and down the sliproad to the tunnel beneath the main road, signed to Weatheroak. Continue 2.5km to a cross-roads, then turn left along Weatheroak Hill. (To avoid the climb to Forhill, go straight ahead at this cross-roads (Brockhill Lane). At the end, turn left and left again.) At the bottom of Weatheroak Hill, turn right by the Coach & Horses, head up Icknield St, and prepare for a low-gear climb (30m up in 500m). The Peacock pub lies at the end of this lane in Forhill on the left.*

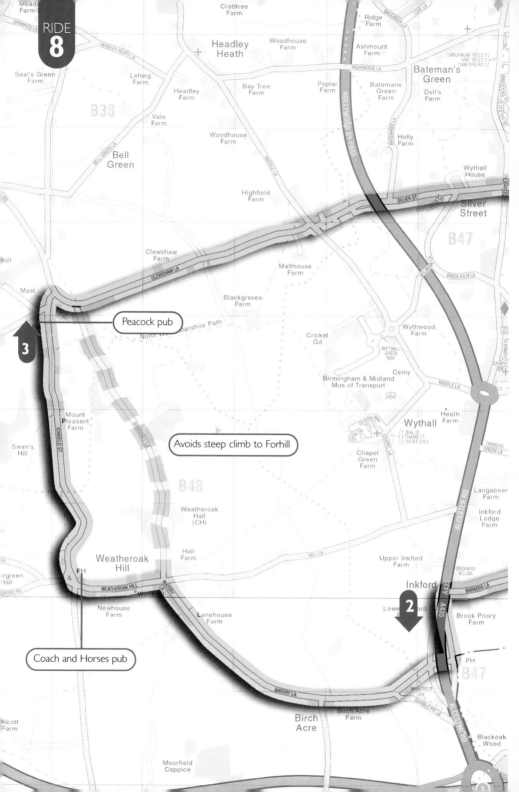

Peacock pub

Avoids steep climb to Forhill

Coach and Horses pub

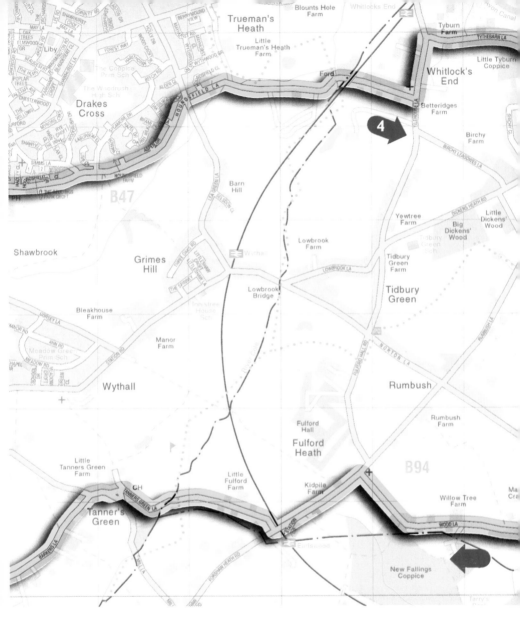

3 At the T-junction go right (signed to Wythall). Continue, with traffic, for 1.5km to a dogleg cross-roads. Continue in the same direction (signed to Wythall) for 1km to another cross-roads. Continue in the same direction (Houndsfield Lane) for 1km to another cross-roads, and continue in the same direction (signed to Shirley) for 1.5km via the ford of the River Cole to a T-junction (Betteridge's Farm).

4 Turn left, and shortly, carefully right at Tythe Barn Lane. Continue for 800m, then, on a right-hand bend amid new housing, bear left on the old road (if you pass the school you have gone too far). Continue to the canal bridge.

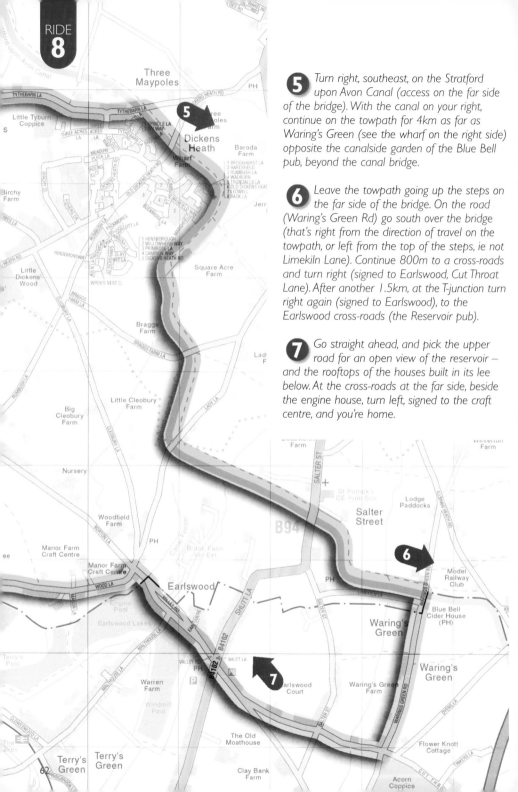

5 Turn right, southeast, on the Stratford upon Avon Canal (access on the far side of the bridge). With the canal on your right, continue on the towpath for 4km as far as Waring's Green (see the wharf on the right side) opposite the canalside garden of the Blue Bell pub, beyond the canal bridge.

6 Leave the towpath going up the steps on the far side of the bridge. On the road (Waring's Green Rd) go south over the bridge (that's right from the direction of travel on the towpath, or left from the top of the steps, ie not Limekiln Lane). Continue 800m to a cross-roads and turn right (signed to Earlswood, Cut Throat Lane). After another 1.5km, at the T-junction turn right again (signed to Earlswood), to the Earlswood cross-roads (the Reservoir pub).

7 Go straight ahead, and pick the upper road for an open view of the reservoir – and the rooftops of the houses built in its lee below. At the cross-roads at the far side, beside the engine house, turn left, signed to the craft centre, and you're home.

Not aerodynamic, but very pretty (Earlswood
Craft Centre).

Bourn Brook & River Rea

via the University & Bournville

A streams and towpath tour of southwest Brum from Woodgate Valley Country Park, on the Worcester & Birmingham Canal towpath to Birmingham University campus and on to Cannon Hill Park, returning via the elegant parkland of Bournville village.

This circuit is not flawless, but it connects some of Birmingham's finest parkland and in so doing, is half car-free.

Go green immediately in Woodgate Valley Country Park (where there is a cafe) to follow the eastward course of Bourn Brook, this is nicest on grassy pathways through California. At Selly Oak jump on to the canal for a short stint to reach the university campus. Thereafter pick up the excellent River Rea cycle route, through lovely Cannon Hill Park (near the Midlands Arts Centre (MAC)

RIDE INFORMATION

Distance 21km (13 miles)
Car-free 10km (6 miles) (48%)

Grade
Moderate – flat, but unsurfaced, and feels longer than the distance suggests because of the variety of sections and navigating between them.

Suitability for children and occasional riders?
Not good as a whole for children, but perfect in sections; Woodgate Valley Country Park, the Cannon Hill Park/River Rea cycle route (continues south to Northfield) and Bournville parkland.

Traffic
There are numerous encounters with traffic; a mixture of crossings over minor roads, and some fast, busy points where less confident cyclists could walk on the pavement – in Selly Oak at the Bristol Rd

(A38) junction; 400m on the Pershore Rd to Cannon Hill Park; crossing lanes in tight traffic in Stirchley on Pershore Rd/Hazelwell Rd/Bournville Lane; also on the road section at the end back to Woodgate Valley Country Park.

Start/finish
Woodgate Valley Country Park Visitor Centre, off Clapgate Lane in Woodgate, southwest Birmingham.

Stations
University, Selly Oak, Bournville.

Refreshments
Cafe at Woodgate Valley Country Park Visitor Centre (open daily all-year round); cafe at the Midlands Arts Centre (Cannon Hill Park).

What to see
The University of Birmingham, featuring the

Woodgate Valley Country Park is good for family cycling.

Chamberlain Tower and the Great Hall designed by Sir Aston Webb and Ingress Bell 1900-09. The tower is nicknamed 'Old Joe'.

Birmingham Nature Centre (tel: 0121 472 7775) is excellent for children. It tells the story of plants, birds, insects and animals, and has a cafe and play area.

The MAC contains a cinema, galleries, bookshop and child-friendly cafe.

Cadbury World (tel: 0121 451 4159), at the Bournville chocolate factory, is aimed at children and chocaholics.

Bournville village was a workers' model village built by the Cadburys, a Quaker family, in the early 20th century. The junior school with its carillon was built in 1902.

Literature
The West Midlands Cycle Route (NCN5) map is available from Sustrans (tel: 0117 929 0888) and shows the full linear route in detail.

For children and chocaholics of all ages.

You get a fine view of 'Old Joe' and the university
from the Worcester & Birmingham canal.

and its child-friendly cafe), then turn south down on the West Midlands Cycle Route (NCN5). At Bournville we turn back westward, through well-tended Bournville Park and follow its green continuation beside the Bourn stream. The last 3km back to Woodgate Valley are utilitarian, on roads with light traffic. Navigating is not difficult, and you can pick up the route at any point. But the surfaces vary greatly, from an earth path beside Bourn Brook through California (which is best after dry weather and unrideable after wet unless you're on a mountain bike) to smooth tarmac in parkland and on the road.

On the Birmingham & Worcester Canal, please give way to other users and observe the Waterways Code, see page 11.

California: the sunshine suburb.

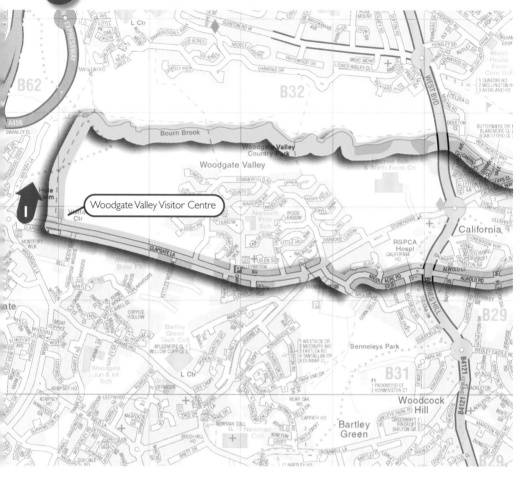

Woodgate Valley Visitor Centre

1 From the bottom corner of the visitor centre car park, follow signs 'to bridleway' past the farm and stables, watching out for walkers and horseriders. Head on down the broad, well-marked track to Bourn Brook at the bottom of the slope. Turn right, eastward, and continue for 2.5km on either the near or far bankside track (the nearside track is official and surfaced for all-weathers), through Woodgate Valley Country Park, and cross West Boulevard to California Way – the park limits.

Cross and continue beside Bourn Brook on the grass track, for 2km (crossing minor roads) to the limit of the brookside track at the main road, Harborne Lane.

2 Turn right (cross carefully), continue to the junction and turn left (Chapel Lane, Sainsbury's on the right), then up to the major junction with the Bristol Rd (A38). Dismount and cross to the far side and take the tarmacked track (the Dingle), which slopes down to the canal (Vauxhall showroom on the right).

At the canal, the Worcester & Birmingham, turn left, northwards (under the bridge) and continue for 1km to the roadbridge over the canal at University station. Leave the canal via the steps. On the road above, University Rd West, turn left into the university campus.

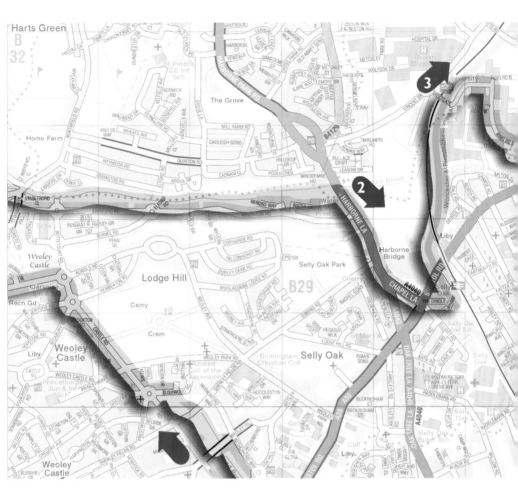

3 Continue to a T-junction, and turn right on the ring road, go anticlockwise through 45° then join concentric Ring Rd South on the right, and continue in the same direction. After 100m (towards the end of the sports pitches), turn right on a road with a cycletrack (no entry to cars), and roll downhill to exit the university at South Gate on the Bristol Road (A38). Cross over and head straight ahead up Bournbrook Rd. Soon take the first left, Oakfield Rd, and continue for 1km to the end, the Pershore Rd. Turn left and continue for 300m, as far the Nature Centre & Museum on the right.

The junior school in Bournville village.

Cannon Hill Park, which like Woodgate Valley, has a cafe.

4 Cross over the road, pass the centre, and head leftwards into the car park. Take the footbridge over the River Rea, and follow signs pointing right (southward) for the River Rea Cycleway (NCN5) through green and pleasant Cannon Hill Park. The MAC and cafe lie 400m left.

Continue beside the river following cycleway signs (the route crosses to the other bank) for 1km. Leave the riverside staying on the NCN5 route via Kitchener Rd/Cecil Rd, cross Dogpool Lane and continue through green parkland for another 1km. Leave the route at the Cartland Rd crossing. (This paragraph overlaps with the South Birmingham green circuit, Route 7.)

5 Turn right on Cartland Rd, back to the main Pershore Rd and turn left, into sticky traffic. Either on the road or walking on the pavement, do a U-turn round the one-way right-hand corner (into Hazelwell St), and take the immediate left, Bournville Lane. Continue for 1km, past the Bournville Works, and go briefly right on Linden Rd.

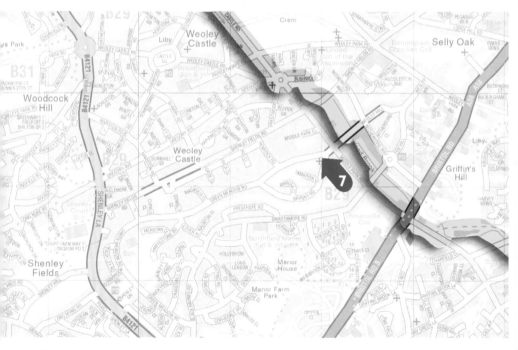

6 Opposite the entrance to Cadbury World turn left into Bournville Park. This is the start of 2km of popular parkland and playing fields along the Bourn stream. Ride mindfully of people and dogs. Cross five minor roads (plus the A38, see below), to the finish at the little lake of Shenley Fields, and Castle Rd roundabout.

The only time you lose sight of the Bourn is after 1km beyond Valley Parkway lake. Turn right on Bournville Lane to the Bristol Rd dual carriageway and cross carefully (towards the right), to regain the parkland path with the stream on your right.

7 This last 3km road section closes the gap as directly as possible back to the start/finish. At Castle Rd roundabout, turn right at the fourth exit (Castle Rd) and continue for 1.5km. Turn left into Alwold Rd for 1km, cross over Barnes Hill into Middle Acre Rd (for 500m), turn right into Mill Lane (200m), then left at Clapgate Lane (1.5km) to Woodgate Valley Country Park Visitor Centre.

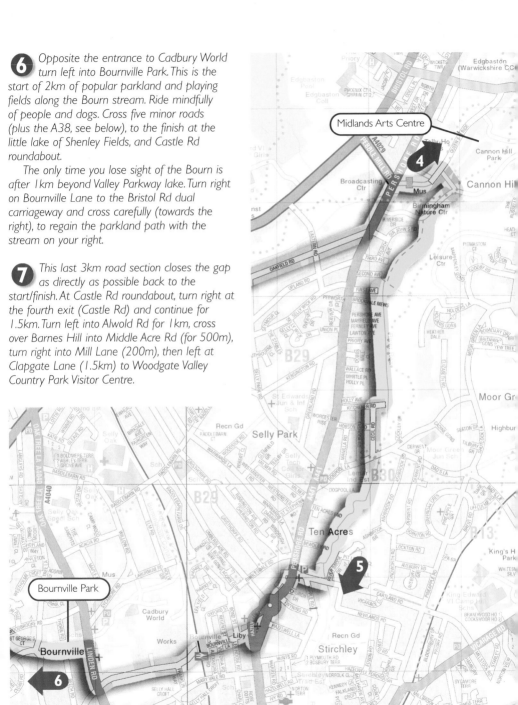

Lickey Hills quickie

RIDE INFORMATION

Distance	10km (6 miles) (plus 1.5km/ 1 mile optional)
Off-road	6.4km (4 miles) (64%)
Grade	Moderate off-road, with a long steady climb

Suitability for children and occasional riders?
Good in part for adventurous children and as an introduction to mountain biking; the ascent requires middling effort.

Traffic
3km on-road, one major crossing.

Start/finish
Lickey Hills Country Park Visitor Centre (tel: 0121 447 7106), off B4096 in the middle of the hills, two miles from both M5 J4 and M42 J2.

Stations
Barnt Green is en route.

Refreshments
Cafe at the visitor centre (open daily all-year round).

Literature
A free pamphlet shows an outline of the area and is available from the visitor centre.

Lying southwest of Birmingham, the 250m-high wooded ridge that is the Lickey Hills Country Park is a small but sweetly formed mountain biking spot. The total bridleway mileage (you mustn't cycle on the footpaths) extends only four miles, but this circuit includes virtually all of that, to showcase the Lickeys' charm and invites a return visit without a guidebook.

A free map from the visitor centre shows more cyclable tracks, but we stick to those marked on the OS Landranger 139 to be on the safe side. The main viewpoint, Beacon Hill, is unfortunately out of bounds to bikes, but if it's views you want, you can walk 400m on a footpath from the visitor centre up to Cofton Hill (260m).

The main circuit starts from the visitor centre, runs off the ridge to the north, spins round lanes and easy off-road tracks to the east, and climbs back up the southern spine to the top. The tracks on the hills are broad and pebbly, and with the exception of the rough initial descent, a breeze. The circuit thus makes a good hook for a beginner mountain biker.

An additional steep and altogether more peppery one-mile circuit on the eastern escarpment is ideal as an aperitif or digestif to the main ride, and won't take an experienced rider long. A fast, short descent is followed by a steady climb, but watch for walkers – and no mad antics thanks.

A great place for a beginner to try out their new mountain bike.

RIDE
10

1
Pass this lake halfway round the circuit.

1 Start from the visitor centre and take the bridleway due north from beside the car park entrance gates (black and yellow with a fire hydrant). The dirt track soon drops steeply downhill, finishing with rough-hewn steps to the B4096 road. Cross the road and continue in the same direction on the track a little to the left (a golf course on the left), becoming tarmac after 600m, exiting on Eachway Lane. Turn right and stay with the road (which becomes Leach Green Lane) for 500m to the B4120 dual carriageway. Turn right, crossing carefully to the far side and continue for 500m to the roundabout.

2 Turn left (Groveley Lane) and take the third right (at the bottom of a slope, on a left-hand bend) into Chestnut Drive. Continue to the end and join the bridleway and ride for 700m (across the end of the Cofton Reservoir). At the end (Cofton Church Lane) turn left and continue for 750m. Go right on the bridleway, past the ponds and through woodland beside Lower Bittell Reservoir. At the lane at the end (Bittell Farm Rd) go right. After 350m, turn right on B4120 Bittell Rd, through Barnt Green and beneath the railway bridge. At the inn (Toby Carvery) beyond, turn left into Cherry Hill Rd. After 500m, turn right on the bridleway and back to the Lickey Hills.

3 Follow the stony track steadily uphill and stay on the best-marked track (ignore crosstracks), after 800m bending right, and straightening up again. At a major track junction (one track leading to the visitor centre), turn left (the mini-circuit comes in from the right) continuing to climb gently. After 250m, at another big junction, fork left towards Twatling Rd (not to the visitor centre – this is to avoid a footpath). After 200m, turn right (not to Twatling Rd) continuing to climb, with a playground on the right, back to the road round to the visitor centre.

4 (A steep extra mini-circuit – watch for walkers and ruts on the descent.) From the visitor centre, follow the signs for Cofton Hill, and stay in the same direction to the end of the car park. Hop over the perimeter log and descend the steep, stony bridleway for 500m to the bottom. Turn right on the road (Barnt Green Rd), continue for 400m, then take the 'Warren St' bridleway back into the woods. Keep straight ahead (don't go right parallel with the road) and curve up round the hill. After 400m, pick up the main route (coming in from the left) and stay right (signed to visitor centre). See instructions in point 3.

74

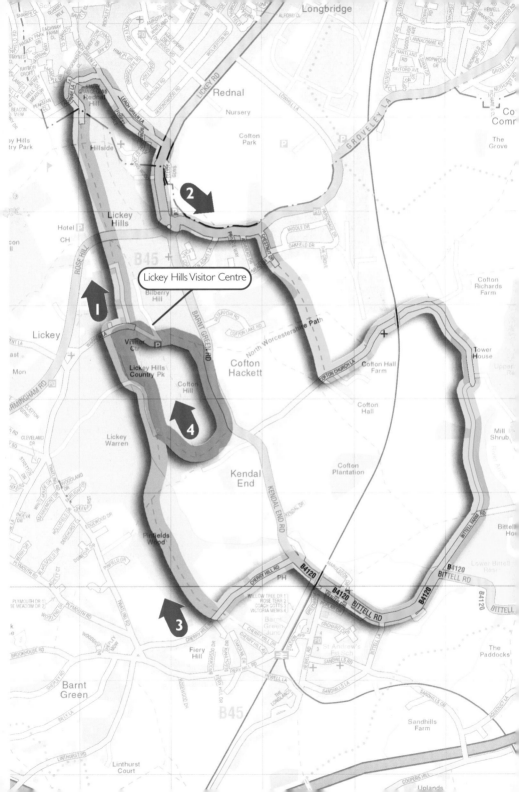

Lickey Hills Visitor Centre

Waseley Hills

and Frankley Beeches

Discover spectacular views, a mountain biking treat and a cake-rich cafe on a short but memorable ride.

The opening salvo of this ride takes your breath away. First, the hill-encircling bridleway delivers a rough, sharp drop. Then it presents the most lung-bursting climb in the book (250m long, 40m up). What's at the top? A set of gorgeous views over to the Malvern Hills and into Wales. Further round see Frankley Beeches, the hilltop stand of trees that burns with colour in the autumn, and is the second goal of the ride.

Relax on tarmac through suburban housing, then ascend gentler Egg Hill to the Beeches.

The traffic on the last 200m rushes by, but among the trees (which are owned by the National Trust), you are a world away. The return leg follows pleasant lanes.

Everything takes place just inside the Worcestershire border and, to point out the obvious, you need a mountain bike and the ability to ride hard under control. After rain, the country park and farm tracks get mucky and slippery. A dry, clear autumn day would be best for the views and colours. The nice cafe at the country park visitor centre is an added charm.

No other cycling is allowed in Waseley Hills Country Park. However, there is a good

RIDE INFORMATION

Distance	10.5km (6½ miles)
Off-road	1.6km (1 mile) (Waseley Hills Country Park – but what a mile)
Grade	Difficult/moderate – the bridleways in the country park are rough and steep.

Suitability for children and occasional riders?
Not suitable, and there's no other cycling in the country park. The road section that gets you to Frankley Beeches carries traffic and contains another hearty climb.

Traffic
Mostly light, briefly bad.

Start/finish
Waseley Hills Country Park.

Station
Longbridge lies 6km east.

Refreshments
Good cafe at Waseley Hills Country Park.

What to see
Stunning high-level views and Frankley Beeches (National Trust).

Literature
There is a general map-guide to the country park. The West Midlands Cycle Route (NCN5) map is available from Sustrans (tel: 0117 929 0888) and shows the full linear route in detail.

You can see all the way to Wales from Waseley
Hill Country Park.

Below: Frankley Beeches, the approach and interior.

adventure playground, plus two walks that cover the compact upland area, and a quick on-foot hike to the top of Windmill Hill for the views. By happy coincidence, the suburban road section utilises part of the West Midlands Cycle Route (NCN5, 160km from Oxford to Derby via Birmingham).

1 *From the country park car park head back out to the road, turn left and then immediately left again up Chapman's Hill. At the farm go straight ahead as the roadway turns into bridleway downhill. Continue for 800m (bumpy, overgrown, slippery in the wet) in the same direction, through several gates and across a concrete roadway, as far as a pair of gates (ahead and on the left) at right-angles on a steep slope. Go through the seven-bar gate on the left and head straight up the field (a bridleway). At the top (views), continue in the same direction through woodland, and out the other side (views). At the end, head right, down a stony doubletrack to houses.*

2 *Turn right at the houses (Gunner Lane), take the first left (Woodlands Rd), and first left again, to join the West Midlands Cycle Route (NCN5) (Hillview Rd/Waseley Rd). Stay with this for 1.5km; at the T-junction turn left (New Inns). At the next junction go straight over and down the pathway, turn right at the bottom (Ormond Rd) and after 200m turn left (Arden Rd). Leave the cycle route (signed right) and stay on Arden Rd to the T-junction at the end. Turn left (New St) and take the second right uphill (Frankley Hill Lane, opposite Frankley High School). Continue for 1km up towards Frankley Beeches, and turn right carefully on to the busy road at the end (Egg Hill Lane) to reach them.*

3 *Retrace your pedalstrokes 500m (back down hill and first left), then turn off right to the smaller lane (Yew Tree Lane, opposite the footpath sign). Stay on this over the M5 to the T-junction. Turn left (Newtown Lane) for 1km to another T-junction, then go left again, back across the M5 to the country park entrance.*

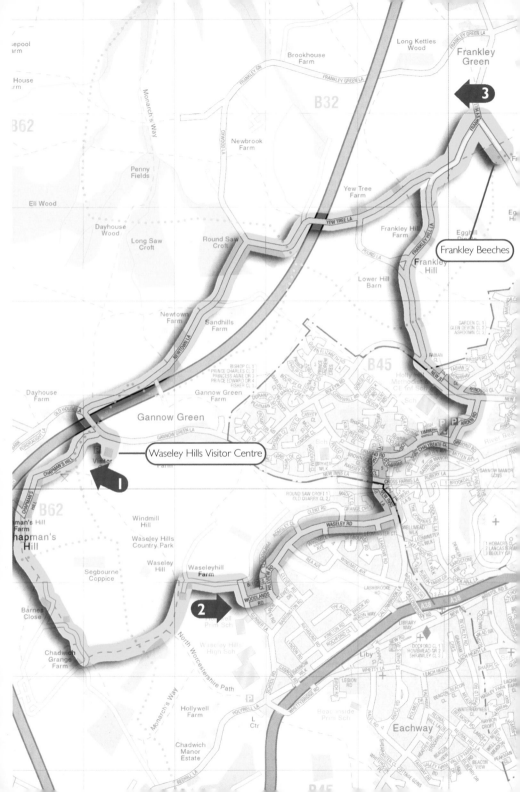

Frankley Beeches

Waseley Hills Visitor Centre

Clent Hills

Mountain biking on the lovely Clent Hills is challenging and rewarding – but you must yield to all other users and take particular care going downhill. Another of the wooded uplands southwest of the conurbation, Clent's slopes and tops are riddled with rideable tracks. The views are outstanding on a clear day when you can see as far as the Black Mountains in Wales, as well as to the Malverns and Clee. The hills are owned and managed by the National Trust and fall inside Worcestershire.

The Ordnance Survey Explorer map of the Clent Hills is shown here, and it is suggested you explore the bridleways at will. They go up and over the summit (300m, the Four Stones and viewpoint), but also circumnavigate the hills by following contouring bridleways, particularly from the Clent village side. If you are a hardy hill-pedaller any combination of riding is possible.

Less fit riders and children can still enjoy the ride up to the summit outlook from Nimmings Wood car park. This is a good place to start anyway, considering the cafe and parking, but you can also ride up into the hills from Clent past either the Hill Tavern or the Vine pub. The next ridge southeast is Walton

RIDE INFORMATION

Distance	9.6km (6 miles) of bridleway
Off-road	100% (excluding lanes to Walton Hill)
Grade	Moderate to difficult

Suitability for children and occasional riders?
From Nimmings Wood car park up to the open outlook point and standing stones is quite hilly, but surmountable. The rest of the riding round the hills is steep and rough in places.

Traffic
Only if you want to cross to Walton Hill, but be wary of vehicles on the narrow, hilly lanes.

Start/finish
Nimmings Wood Visitor Centre car park,

off the minor road signed from the A456 Hagley road (just inside Worcestershire).

Stations
Hagley lies 4km west (as the crow flies).

Refreshments
Cafe at Nimmings Wood Visitor Centre, the Hill Tavern on the southwest slope, and the Vine pub on the southeast slope on the yellow road which bisects the hills southwest/northeast.

Literature
There is no country park map, other than an orienteering sheet.

The local office of the National Trust is on tel: 01684 855336/855300.

Top: The cafe and visitor centre at Nimmings Wood.

Bottom: Watch out for all the other people enjoying the hills.

www.stourbridge.com

RIDE **12**

Bogs Wood

Hagley Wood

Hagley Wood Lane

Hagley Hill Farm Barns

Spring Farm

Resr

Moor Lane

P

Hagley Park

Nimmings Plantation

267

Nimmings Wood Visitor Centre

Chapel Farm

Short Wood

Penorchard Farm

219

232

94

265

North Worcestershire Path

The Four Stones

High Harcourt Farm

264

239

254

Hill Tavern

P

223

315

Clent Hills Country Park

Deep Wood

St Kenelm's Pass

Holt Lane

Spring Lane

Whitehall Farm

Adam's Hill

Dark Pool

Walton Hill

Rumbow Lane

176

Nag Hill

Clent Hills

Waltonhill Farm

163

Clent

Vic

Vine pub

CLENT C P

Rumbow Cottages

201

Walton Pool

225

Spr

FB

Shut Mill Lane

PO Sch

Mousehole Farm

190

Walton House

163

Walton Farm

Squats Wood

Calcot Hill

Calcothill Farm

Clent Grange

149

Spr

Moorhall Farm

210

Stourbridge

ite Lodge Farm

FB

Weirs

156

Explore the bridleways of the Clent Hills, as indicated by the green dashed lines

Hill (298m), accessible by lanes from the country park to bridleways approaching both southwest and north.

Watch out for all the other people enjoying the hills; walkers and dogs particularly, also children and horseriders: especially when riding downhill over ruts and bumps, and in the woods. Say 'hello' and 'thank you' and keep cyclists welcome in the Clent Hills.

Right: The Vine pub on the southeast slope.

Below: Head for the viewpoint at the summit near the four stones.

www.stourbridge.com

Sandwell Valley Country Park and canal circuit

RIDE INFORMATION

Distance	20km (12½ miles)
Car-free	18.5km (11½ miles) 93% (country park and towpaths)
Grade	Moderate (although nearly all flat, most of the towpath along the Tame Valley Canal is unsurfaced, narrow and rutted).

Suitability for children and occasional riders?
Sandwell Valley Country Park is eminently suited to children and pootlers, especially considering it has two farms. But long sections of unsurfaced canal towpath are rutted and muddy after rain, which makes the circuit as a whole only suitable for more experienced riders with mountain bikes.

Traffic
Where there is any cycling on the road, we follow segregated cycle lanes and crossings on the National Cycle Network Route 5.

Start/finish
Sandwell Park Farm (or Forge Mill Farm).

Stations
Tame Bridge, Smethwick, Galton Bridge, Sandwell & Dudley.

Refreshments
Tearooms at Sandwell Park Farm.

What to see
Lakeside scenes in Sandwell Valley Country Park, plus rare breeds animal farm and the old kitchen garden at Sandwell Park Farm. At nearby Forge Mill Farm you can visit a working modern dairy farm, view the Jersey cows being milked and feed the hens and goats. (Some people may also find close-up views of the M5 and M6 motorways a bit of a thrill.)

Literature
A good large-scale walking/cycling map of Sandwell Valley Country Park shows bridleways not marked on any other map. Free from Park Farm (tel: 0121 553 0220).

The Birmingham Canal Navigations map (Geoprojects, 9 Southern Court, South St, Reading RG1 4QS, tel: 0118 939 3567) gives full details of the towpaths, plus historical information.

The West Midlands Cycle Route (NCN5) map is available from Sustrans (tel: 0117 929 0888) and shows the full linear route in detail.

Soon after the start, head off up the River Tame on NCN5.

A parkland and towpath circuit with views, open spaces and canal features. The start/finish at 18th-century Sandwell Park Farm is a treat, with a cafe, rare breed pigs and shire horses!

The star of this circuit is Sandwell Park Farm, the handsome redbrick 18th-century model farm where you can get a cuppa and admire the Gloucester Old Spot pigs. The surrounding country park generally offers quite a bit of cycling, made up of mini MTB circuits and a section of NCN5. If you have children or pootlers, there's no need to leave the park.

The canal sections are open and rideable, and although less scenic they feature interesting structures and tempt exploration by mountain bike. So, for the adventurous, we go north through the country park beside the River Tame on NCN5 to the Tame Valley Canal towpath. This leads in a more or less straight line for 5km to the Walsall Canal, (although at one point you do have to cross

to the far bank via a high bridge with 40 steps on each side). On the Walsall Canal you pass the seven-number Ryders Green Locks en route for the New Main Line Canal.

Here are the most interesting waterway features (on a section which overlaps with the Main Line Circuit, see page 92). First comes the M5 with its feet in the water. Just beyond is Thomas Telford's grand 21m deep canal cutting, the Galton Valley. Now appearing natural it was then the largest earthwork in the world crossed by the largest single-span bridge, the cast-iron Galton Bridge. Here, ascend the bank on a special cycle path to follow the NCN route back to Sandwell Valley Country Park.

The British Waterways office for the region sits beside Tame Valley Junction and you are welcome to pop in to reception for literature and information. As with all towpath riding, give way to all other users and observe the Waterways Code (see page 11). There are a couple of smooth brick ramps serving bridges where you need to ride carefully under control (especially in rain), and low bridges which should be tackled with care. Note that the anti-motorbike barriers on the towpaths are awkward at the best of times, and very hard to negotiate with trailerbikes, panniers or recumbents. These barriers occur intermittently.

People with bikes on the car roof rack – beware height restrictions on entry to Sandwell Valley Country Park!

Mountain Biking in Sandwell Valley Country Park

Sandwell Valley qualifies as a little mountain bike destination in its own right, with routes and general facilities.

Two short mountain bike circuits have been set out and signposted (see the free walking/cycling map), each about 1.5km long. There is also about 6.5km of bridleway marked on the country park map (which do not appear on the Ordnance Survey Landranger 31 map of the region).

Sandwell Valley is a fixture on the mountain biking calendar as the venue for the annual midsummer 24-hour endurance race, Red Bull Mountain Mayhem.

1 At the top left-hand corner of the car park at Sandwell Park Farm, head along the path for 100m to join NCN5 where it comes in from the right. Following the NCN5 signs from here all the way to the Tame Valley Canal, continue straight ahead over the motorway bridge, and don't miss the immediate left-hand turn on the far side. Continue to Swan Pool, take the route round the left bank to the yachting club, turn left behind the buildings and find the track right again, over the road and through bushes to the car park for Forge Mill Farm.

2 Head right to the lake (Balancing Lake) and turn left along the right-hand bank of the River Tame (signed to Walsall). Continue

beside that (following the NCN5 signs) for 1.5km, to the lane beneath the road bridge. Stay with the signs; go right then immediately left up Ray Hall Lane, then right back on to the track. Continue to the Tame Valley Canal towpath and turn left (west) where signed to Walsall.

3 Continue under the bridges, and keep straight ahead on the unsurfaced left bank towpath of the Tame Valley Canal (here, NCN5 heads over the canal bridge and off right, north, up Rushall Canal). Stay with the Tame Valley Canal for 5km, as far as the Tame Valley Junction at Ocker Hill, the site of the British Waterways office.

The towpath jumps banks after 2km (via a

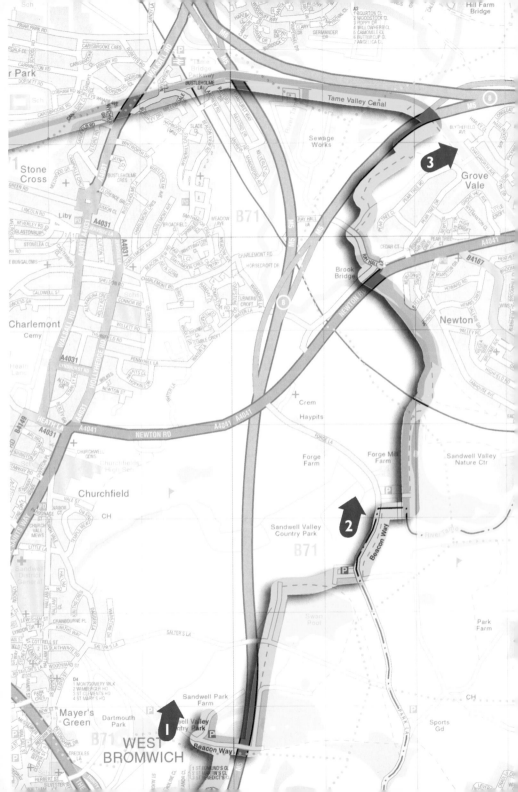

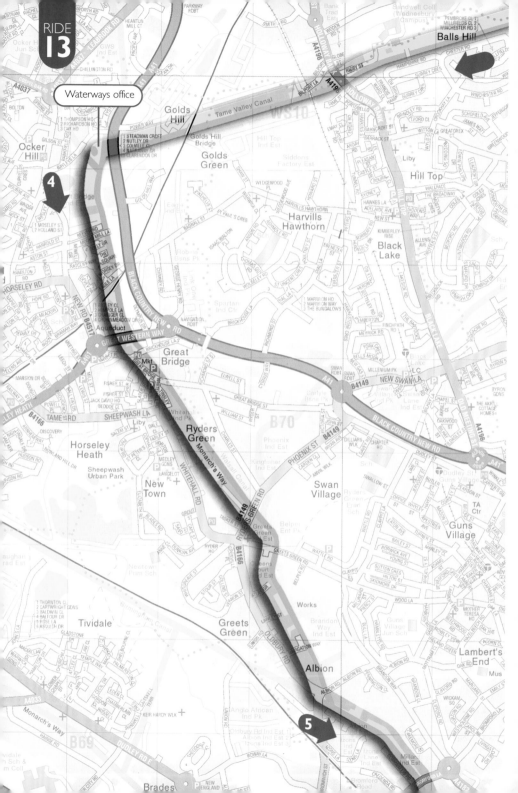

high road bridge over the canal, with 40 steps up and down) and is then better surfaced for a short while. Otherwise, this towpath is a bit rutted, and, after rain, is quite muddy most of the way.

4 At Tame Valley Junction go over the bridge and left, south (over a second bridge across the closed Ocker Hill Tunnel branch), along the Walsall Canal, signed for Ryders Green Junction. Continue for 2km, climbing beside the seven-strong flight of locks at Ryders Green to Ryders Green Junction (where the Wednesbury

Old Canal, goes off left, north). Continue for 800m to Pudding Green Junction.

5 Turn left, signed for Birmingham, joining the New Main Line Canal Cycleway. After 800m, you reach Bromford Junction (the fork where the Old Main Line goes off left via Spon Lane Locks). Keep straight ahead on the New Main Line (beneath the M5 motorway piers), switching to the left bank. Continue for 1.5km, via Galton Valley to Galton Bridge and Galton Tunnel.

The view back over the River Tame from the elevated Tame Valley Canal.

Feeding the birds at the canal junction at Ocker Hill. The Waterways office is off to the right.

6 Rejoin the NCN5 cycle route on roads back to the country park. First, take the challenge of climbing all the way up the bank on the zigzag cyclepath, to the end of Galton Bridge. Turn right at the top of the bank (Roebuck Lane), along the path to the roundabout, go a quarter way round on the pavement, then cross, right, over the cycle crossing. Keep straight ahead, beneath the M5, and along Roebuck Lane

residential street. At the top, turn right on the pavement cycle lane (Birmingham Rd) for 200m, as far as the left turn (Beeches Rd). Turn right after 150m (Europa Ave), right again at the T-junction and round anticlockwise for 160°, then right into St John's Close which is a dead end – don't miss this turn. Back in the country park, at the pathway T-junction, turn left for Sandwell Park Farm.

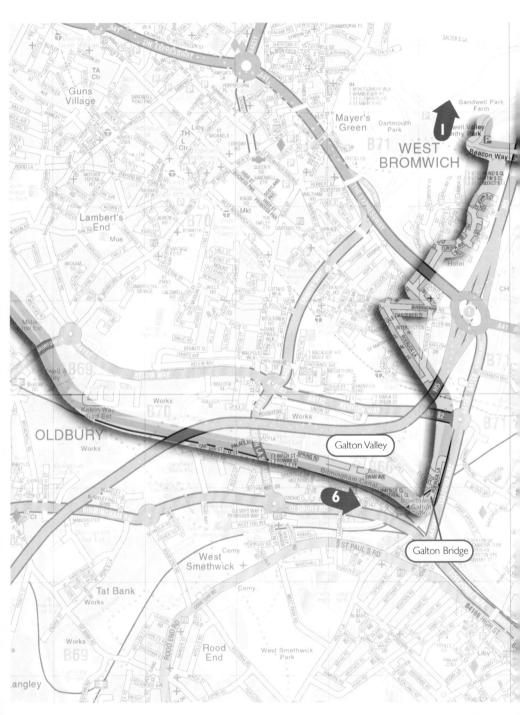

New and Old Line canal tour

This classic canal circuit explores the parallel courses of the Old and New lines of the Birmingham to Wolverhampton Main Line waterway, once a thronging highway between the two centres. It is entirely without traffic, packed with features and partly uses the upgraded Main Line Cycleway. The parallel railway line makes it easy to join and depart.

This rewarding route transports you peacefully for 20km (12 miles) around the built-up heart of Birmingham and the Black Country.

Most of the towpath is in good condition, although a short section at the start of the Old Main Line is unsurfaced and rough. (British Waterways hopes to have the entire Old Main Line towpath surfaced eventually.) Generally, the path on the New Main Line on the return leg is better, as it is part of the Main Line Canal Cycleway.

A good place to eat and drink at the turnaround point is the recommended Pie Factory (see Refreshments), while the canalside Barge & Barrel pub nearby has outside tables.

Give way and be friendly to all other towpath users, and follow the Waterways Code, see page 11. Note that the anti-

RIDE INFORMATION

Distance	20km (12½ miles)
Car-free	100%
Grade	Easy to moderate, all flat with a couple of narrow, rough patches.

Suitability for children and occasional riders?
Eminently suitable from the point of view of flatness and interest, but children must have good bike control to ride safely beside the water, and to enjoy themselves over a dozen short but bumpy patches.

Traffic   None

Start/finish & parking
In Smethwick, at the Galton Valley Canal Heritage Centre (Brasshouse Lane, just off the A457 in Smethwick, with car park) at the southeastern turnaround point. The Black Country Museum (Tipton Rd, Dudley), near the northwestern turnaround point, has parking, but watch the height restriction.

Stations
Smethwick Rolfe St, Smethwick Galton Bridge, Sandwell & Dudley, Dudley Port, Tipton.

Refreshments
Soft drinks cabinet only at Galton Valley Canal Heritage Centre; Smethwick High Street is renowned for its Asian sweetshops; the Pie Factory at Tipton is an institution, serving delicious Black Country fare (200m left, south of the canal at Factory Junction, the turnaround point at the road junction with Sedgeley Road West); the Barge & Barrel pub (Factory Junction itself); the fish and chips served in the Black Country

The fine Telford Aqueduct, which feeds water into the canal from Edgbaston Reservoir.

Museum are worthy of a full museum visit, but in the meantime, you are allowed to eat at the cafe without paying the museum entrance fee.

What to see
The Galton Valley Canal Heritage Centre at Smethwick (Brasshouse Lane, tel: 0121 558 8195) is a small museum devoted to the history of the canals and canal life. The neighbouring canalside Smethwick Pumping Station has been restored and is open to visitors by arrangement.

The Black Country Museum (Tipton Rd, Dudley, tel: 0121 557 9643) is a 26-acre open-air museum with original buildings and tableaux from the region's industrial heyday, including a Victorian school, coal mine, shops and tramcar rides.

Dudley Tunnel canal excursions travel the length of the 2,888m tunnel between

Dudley and Tipton, and visit the extraordinary limestone caverns inside. 45-minute trips (which include an underground audio-visual show) run Easter-October, and you have to book in advance (tel: 01384 236275; website: www.dudleycanaltrust. org.uk).

Literature
The Birmingham Canal Navigations map is a good aid to understanding the canals, and shows clearly how the old and new main lines interweave (available from GeoProjects, 9 Southern Court, South St, Reading RG1 4QS, tel: 0118 939 3567).

For literature on the Galton Valley section of the route, the British Waterways visitor information centre in Gas Street Basin (tel: 0121 632 6845) has a full and fascinating selection of waterways literature.

When Telford constructed the Galton Bridge it was the longest single-span bridge in the world.

Smethwick pumping station lies between the Old and New lines, and opens by arrangement.

motorbike barriers on the towpaths are awkward at the best of times, and very hard to negotiate with trailerbikes, panniers or recumbents. They occur intermittently.

The Birmingham & Black Country Canal Cycleway

This is a part-upgraded section of canal that runs for 22.5km (14 miles) between Birmingham and Wolverhampton. It connects very well with the corresponding railway route, so you can hop on and hop off where you will.

The Old and New Main Line canals

Learn through riding them why and how the narrow, meandering Old Main Line, built by James Brindley in 1769, was surpassed 70 years later by Thomas Telford's broad, straight New Main Line in 1838. It is their separate but related courses that make our circuit.

The first canal followed the contours of the land using locks to deal with unavoidable elevations and depressions. But at the turn of the 18th/19th centuries, industry was booming, the canals did much of the transport work and the locks were causing congestion on this critical waterway. Relief came in the shape of Telford's deep cutting through the Smethwick summit (which Brindley surmounted with 12 locks) to create Galton Valley – whose V-shape has long been recolonised by mature vegetation and appears natural. Galton Valley was then the largest earthwork in the world, crossed by Galton Bridge, the world's longest single-span bridge at the time. Using more cuttings and embankments Telford cut a total of 11km (7 miles) off the course of the old canal between Birmingham and Wolverhampton.

Canal features

Throughout the trip canal sights are plentiful. From the start we initially head southeast on the Old Main Line past John Smeaton's Smethwick Locks and Telford's fine Engine Arm Aqueduct (which carries the feeder channel from Edgbaston Reservoir), as far as Smethwick Junction. Here, we turn back parallel to ourselves on the New Main Line, now passing beneath the Engine Arm Aqueduct. We continue through Galton Tunnel, beneath Galton Bridge and into Galton Valley.

Where the Old Main Line later branches off left, southwest from the New Main Line, the M5 motorway stands with its feet in the water. The Old canal jumps in and out from beneath the motorway for a while, then heads northwest towards Dudley, via a two-rung ladder of canals that link to the parallel New Canal, one of which also serves the entrance to the Netherton Tunnel (1858, 4km long). This wide bore, gaslit tunnel has a towpath either side and was built to relieve the older Dudley Tunnel (3km long).

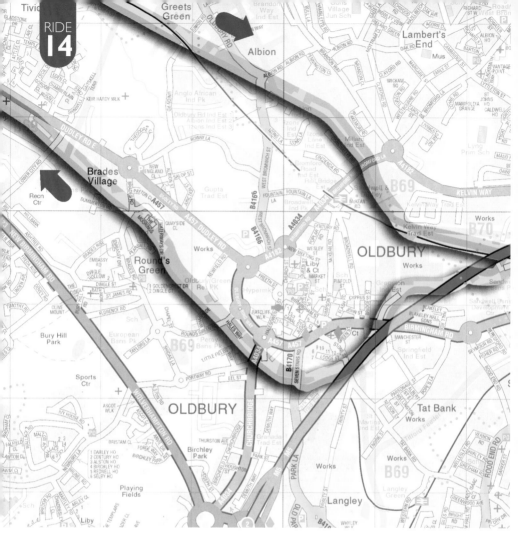

1 From the Galton Valley Canal Heritage Centre head down the road to the canal bridge, and turn left carefully down the brick-paved slope to the upper left-hand canal, the Old Main Line (the lower right-hand canal is the New Main Line, which comes later), opposite the new housing up on the bank (signed to Birmingham). Follow this (east) past the picturesque Smethwick Locks and Engine Arm Aqueduct, and continue 800m. As the towpath deteriorates sharply, and you have to watch a drop down beneath a bridge to Smethwick Junction, although British Waterways has scheduled this section for improvement.

2 Don't cross any bridges. Do a U-turn on to the well-surfaced Main Line Cycleway (duplicating the West Midlands National Cycle Route NCN 5) back, parallel with the way you have come, and on the New Main Line (signed to Wolverhampton). Continue for an interesting 3km, beneath the Engine Arm Aqueduct, through Galton Tunnel (here the NCN5 leaves the canal, going right up the bank, see Sandwell Valley, Route 13), beneath Telford's Galton Bridge and through the naturalised Galton Valley. At the bridge just this side of the M5 motorway, with its columns in the centre of the canal, climb right up a brick-paved zigzag ramp to the canal above, an aqueduct for the Old Main Line.

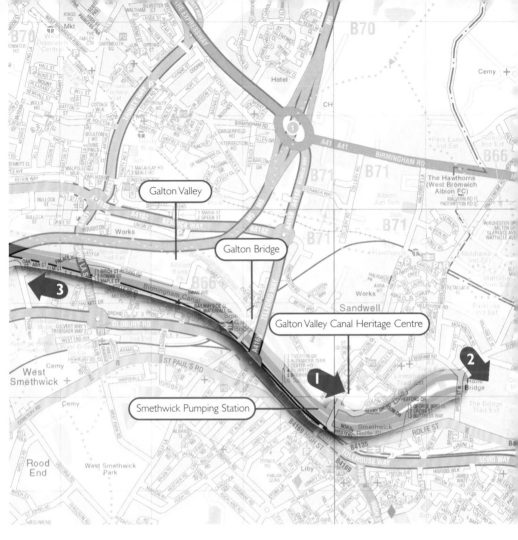

3 Turn left (cross over the top of the New Main Line Canal), now on the Old Main Line Canal (the waterway on your right initially). You follow this for a total of 6.5km to Factory Junction in Tipton (landmarked by the Barge & Barrel pub).

En route: After about 200m, cross over the second bridge (Blakeley Hall Bridge) to the right bank, through the motorway columns (the canal now on your left). After 800m, at Oldbury Junction, stay on the towpath and continue. 800m further on, the Gower Branch on your right is the first link to the New Main Line. Another 800m after that, at Dudley Port (100 miles from the sea) comes the

Netherton Tunnel Branch and, to the left, the entrance to the Netherton Tunnel

After another 1.5km comes Tipton Junction (with the Dudley Tunnel Approach coming in from the left). Continue right unless you want to visit the Black Country Museum. (For this, leave the towpath 800m before Factory Junction. The museum is signposted from the towpath; go left over Pitchfork Bridge, stay on the towpath round the left-hand corner (Tipton Junction into what is Dudley Tunnel Approach). Leave at the road bridge before the tunnel, cross Birmingham New Rd and head straight up the main Tipton Road.)

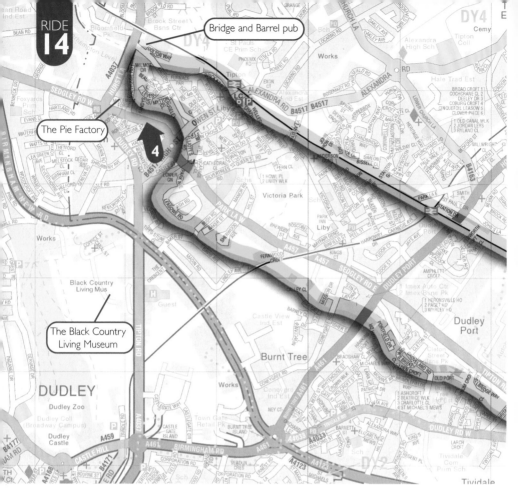

RIDE 14

- Bridge and Barrel pub
- The Pie Factory
- **4**
- The Black Country Living Museum

4 At Factory Junction, cross the bridge to the New Main Line, and turn right to head southeast, past Factory Locks. Stay on the New Main Line for 8km all the way back (in a much straighter line) to Smethwick and the finish. This section follows the Main Line Cycleway and is well surfaced in places, less so in others. Follow signs to cross to the far bank at times.

The first 5km are largely featureless, then everything comes at once nearing the M5 legs. At Bromford Junction, a connecting branch forks left up Spon Lane Locks to the Old Main Line, although we keep going straight ahead, merely jumping to the left bank to continue to the M5 columns. Retrace your steps back to the start.

At the end there is a good pedalling challenge; a stiff climb up a zigzag slope from the canal, back up to Brasshouse Lane.

Where the New (left) and Old (right) Main Lines meet (point 2).

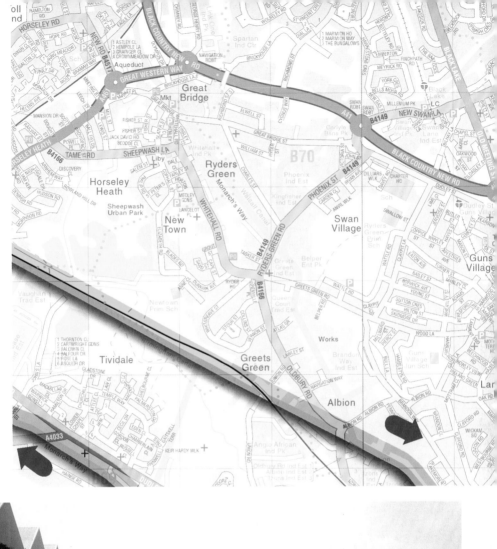

Dudley Canals

from Windmill End

to the Waterfront

Contrast historic and modern canalsides on a fascinating out-and-back trip that waggles round the hillside. These are the Dudley Nos 1 and 2 canals, starting from the Netherton Tunnel, and passing the entrance to Dudley Tunnel then turning round at the modernistic Waterfront at Merry Hill.

This nippy canal jaunt is packed with historic features and feels surprisingly rural in places

along Dudley's green ridgeline. The route lies at the heart of the area from which the Black Country got its name. The slopes were once riddled with coal, iron ore and fire clay mines, and are now notorious for subsidence. The Dudley Nos 1 and 2 canals were built to serve the mines and works, and, via two tunnels, they connect with the Birmingham to Wolverhampton Main Line Canal on the far side

RIDE INFORMATION

Distance	14.5km (9 miles) return
Car-free	100% (all towpath)
Grade	Easy-moderate (towpath rough and narrow in places).

Suitability for children and occasional riders?
Good for children if their bike control can be trusted as the route is entirely beside water. Unfit riders will like the short distance and flat gradient, but the towpath is a little rough in places.

Traffic
None

Start/finish
There are two places. The first is at the Dry Dock pub, Windmill End (near the mouth of the Netherton Tunnel); from Halesowen Rd turn in to Cole St, then Darby End Rd at Windmill End. The other is at the Waterfront, Merry Hill.

Station
Old Hill lies southeast along Dudley No. 2 Canal at Blackheath, 2.5km by towpath from the start at Windmill End.

Refreshments
At the start is the Dry Dock pub (which has a narrowboat in the bar) and the Bumble Hole Visitor Centre (snacks and fizzy drinks only), there are modern pubs at the Waterfront at the turnaround point; recommended by the local cycling officer is the Vine pub in Delph Rd at the bottom of the Nine Locks, which brews Bathams beer at the back.

What to see
See next page for canal features, also Bumble Hole Conservation Group Visitor Centre (tel: 01384 814100) at Windmill End has wildlife displays.

Dudley Tunnel canal excursions travel through the tunnel between Dudley and

At the start of the ride, Windmill Hill and Bumble Hole are fascinating places to visit.

Tipton and visit the large limestone caverns. Trips last 45 minutes, run Easter-October and you have to book in advance. Also, Blowers Green Pumphouse has occasional open days with demonstrations of canal arts and crafts as well as boat trips to the Waterfront at Merry Hill. (For both, tel: 01384 236275; website www.dudleycanaltrust.org.uk).

Literature
The Birmingham Canal Navigations map is an excellent aid for understanding the canals (available from GeoProjects, 9 Southern Court, South St, Reading RG1 4QS, tel: 0118 939 3567).

Dudley Council produces two interesting walking leaflets (to Bumble Hole, and to Blackbrook Valley) with historic details covering the route. Also useful is their map of the local cycling network (tel: 01384 815433).

of the hill. We start near the entrance of the later Netherton Tunnel at Windmill End (also known as Bumble Hole) and pass the entrance of the earlier Dudley Tunnel as we progress to the modern waterfront at Merry Hill.

En route are a dozen canal sights, plus, unusually for waterways, long views. The canals lie halfway up the bowl of hills that overlook the Stour Valley. Above is Netherton Hill topped by prominent St Andrews Church (1830). This hillside is now part of Saltwells Wood Local Nature Reserve (tel: 01384 812795). Across the valley to the south is Wychbury Hill. Just visible is Frankley Beeches (see Route 11) to the southeast.

There is no footbridge over the canal at Blowers Green Junction (the only way over is on the lock gate carrying your bike – very tricky and British Waterways won't condone it) which means before we get there we jump on to the road to cross to the No. 1 Canal for a quick ride back to the junction (to see Parkhead Locks and the entrance to Dudley Canal).

Please give way to other users and observe the Waterways Code (see page 11). Note that the anti-motorbike barriers on the

Once blackened by industry, Windmill End and
Bumble Hole are now devoted to conservation.

Cobb's Engine House kept the hillside mines open by keeping the water levels down.

towpaths are awkward at the best of times, and very hard to negotiate with trailerbikes, panniers or recumbents. These barriers occur intermittently.

From our turnaround point at the Waterfront, it's nice also to continue along Dudley No. 1 Canal for 800m to Delph locks, and for a further 4.5km to Leys Junction which connects with the Stourbridge Canal detailed in Route 16, Kingswinford and Stourbridge.

Canal features
Windmill End Junction and Bumble Hole Local Nature Reserve

This patch at the start was once busy with mines extracting the 9m thick seam of the South Staffordshire coalfield. Now a twittering nature reserve, only the ghosts of this major upheaval remain, such as the grassed-over spoil heap of the former Warren Hall Colliery behind Cobb's Engine House (see below).

The four footbridges were built around 1830. The canal crossroads they serve is made up of the Dudley No. 2 Canal (which we follow westward, and which continues southeast round the ridgeline to Coombeswood); the Boshboil Arm (which connected with the Bumble Hole Arm, the original contour canal), and the Netherton Tunnel approach.

Cobb's Engine House at Windmill End

Built in 1831, this evocative landmark performed a critical task pumping water out of the hillside mines to keep them open. After a century in action, the last pit closed in 1928 and the engine house parts were broken up or sold for scrap. Only the 30m chimney stack and winding house have been preserved, now safely in council ownership. An engine house leaflet is available from Sandwell Council (tel: 0121 569 4022).

Highbridge and Brewin's Tunnel Section

At 2km, this deep cutting below a high bridge was originally a tunnel. This was opened and widened in 1858, and is now a classic geological site by dint of exposed carboniferous and silurian rocks.

Two Lock line

At 3km, you cross a cast-iron bridge which used to mark the start of a short link canal that cut the corner between the Nos 1 and 2 canals. Major subsidence closed it in 1909, and subsequent coal workings obliterated its presence.

The route starts off heading this way, past the visitor centre on the left.

The modernistic Waterfront development is a striking contrast to the rest of the historic local canal network.

Parkhead Locks and Dudley Canal entrance

At 4km (halfway) we come to Blowers Green Junction. This serves Parkhead Locks which lead to the mouth of the Dudley Tunnel. Seeing the holding pools, you can imagine the bustle as the narrowboats and folk awaited passage through the tunnel. Narrowboat tunnel trips are operated, see details above.

The Tunnels

The original Dudley Tunnel (1792, 2690m, on No. 1 Canal) has no towpaths and took 2.5 hours to leg through. The later Netherton Tunnel (1858, 2768m, on No. 2 Canal) was built to ease pressure on the Dudley Tunnel with towpaths either side. It turned out to be the last canal tunnel to be built in the country. (There is no cycling through this.)

The entrance to the Dudley Tunnel must have been a disheartening sight for the men about to 'leg' through it for over two hours.

The Parkhead Locks were where boats queued up to go through the Dudley Tunnel.

Find shiny steel structures and drinking holes at the Merry Hill Waterfront.

RIDE
15

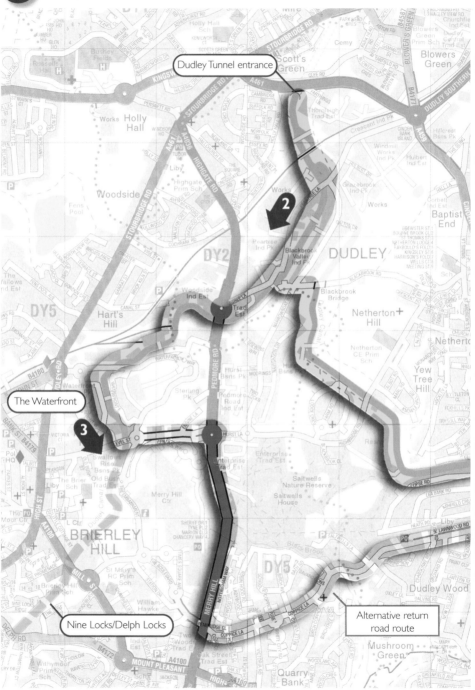

Dudley Tunnel entrance

The Waterfront

Nine Locks/Delph Locks

Alternative return road route

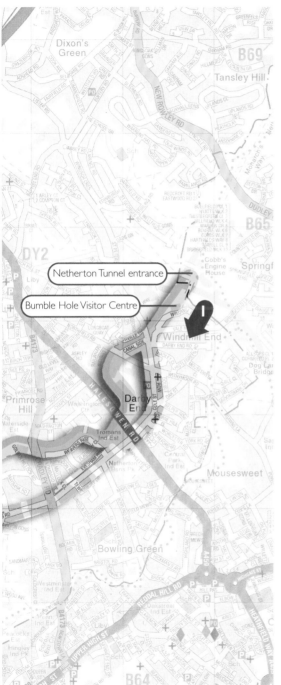

1 From beside the Dry Dock pub, climb up the broad track (signed Bumble Hole Wardens & Visitor Centre) to the canal crossroads at Windmill End Junction (with Cobb's Engine House ahead). Turn left on the towpath of Dudley No. 2 Canal, signed for Merry Hill (see Bumble Hole Visitor Centre on your left). Continue for 3.25km (until 800m after High Bridge, 250m after the Two Lock Line).

2 At Blackbrook Bridge, leave the canal up to Blackbrook Rd. Turn left, cross straight over Narrowboat Way, take the access on the right (Peartree Lane Bridge) then on to Dudley No. 1 Canal. Turn right on the towpath (with the canal on your left) and continue for 600m (cross the canal once) to Blowers Green Junction. At the junction, continue on the towpath alongside Parkhead Locks under the viaduct to the entrance to Dudley Tunnel. Return to the junction and retrace your steps from there (signed Brierley Hill/Black Delph Junction) for 3km to Merry Hill Waterfront. At the Waterfront, dismount to explore the modernised canal basin.

3 From the Waterfront you have three options:
• Continue along Dudley No. 1 Canal past the Waterfront on the embankment south to Nine Locks/Delph Locks (pubs on Delph Road at the bottom lock, see refreshments).
• Return to Windmill End along the canal the way you have come.
• Return to Windmill End quickly on a straightforward but busy road route; drop down to the busy A4036 Merry Hill road, after 500m go left on Coppice Lane – go 2km and then straight ahead (at Halesowen Rd) into Cole St – go 500m right into Darby End Rd and turn left at Windmill End.

Kingswinford rail trail

& Stourbridge Canal

A recommended scenic circuit, of great historic interest, best on a mountain bike.

No cars, plenty of pretty places and a wealth of industrial history. That sums up this circular rail trail and towpath tour through the western outskirts of the conurbation. It is packed with cuttings, locks and bridges as you pass from urban Dudley into the Staffordshire countryside. For your bevvy of choice, pick from the charming cafe in old Wombourne station at the start/finish, and three canalside pubs.

You can ride it on an ordinary bike, but a mountain bike is better. Most of the route is at

---

RIDE INFORMATION

Distance	26km (16 miles)
Car-free	25.5km (15 miles) (98%)
Grade	Moderate, flat but substantial, especially with stops for views and features.

Suitability for children and occasional riders?

It is good for children, being a flat route, but they must have good bike control to ride on the towpaths: and watch those chutes under bridges. The distance is a lot to cope with, so with little ones the route is appropriate only in sections. The same applies for infrequent cyclists.

Traffic

100m worth at the end at Bratch Locks.

Start/finish

On the Kingswinford rail trail at old Wombourne station, near Bratch Locks (watch the height restriction if you have bikes on the roof); alternatively, go 2km off-route at the Bonded Warehouse on the Stourbridge Town Arm (easy to get to from Stourbridge Town station). Follow the Town Arm northwest to the Stourbridge Arm at

Leys Junction to pick up the route.

Stations

Stourbridge – 2km southeast of the Stourbridge Canal near the glass museum.

Refreshments

The cafe at the start/finish; Samson & Lion pub at Buckpool (at 13km); The Navigation pub at Greensforge (at 20km); the Round Oak at Ounsdale (at 25km).

What to see

The Red House Glass Cone Museum & Visitor Centre on the Stourbridge Canal (tel: 01384 812750, High St, Wordsley, open Easter–October 10am–5pm, winter 10am–4pm, £3/£2.50 adults/children over 5). Built in 1790, the Redhouse Cone is the only one left in the Black Country, and is now owned by Stuart Crystal.

Literature

Dudley MBC (tel: 01384 814189) has two free walking leaflets that explain numerous industrial heritage sights including the Pensnett Railway and Blackpool and Fens Pools.

The rail trail is leafy and popular with walkers.

least gravelled, but the rail trail is rough in places, especially after rain, and the descent at Fens Pools is purely off-road.

For our purposes, the route starts at the rail trail at Wombourne (near Bratch Locks), but you can pick it up anywhere you like, eg Himley, Fens Pools, or the Red House Glass Cone Museum.

The first 8km head south and east on the Kingswinford rail trail through nice varied woodland and cuttings, under interesting bridges and up the 1:24 Barrow Hill Incline

where locomotives were once hauled up by a stationary engine. At the end you emerge to overlook Fens Pools, a set of stepped reservoirs built to feed the canal and now a verdant nature reserve rich with waterfowl.

We are now waterside to the end. Beyond the pools comes the towpath of the characterful narrow Stourbridge Canal and its drop of 16 manicured locks. At the bottom is the Red House Glass Cone Museum. After 6km, we turn on to the Staffordshire and Worcestershire Canal for the 10km

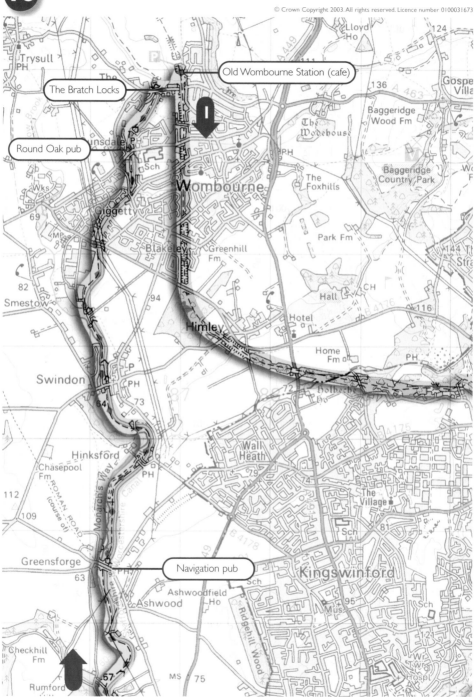

RIDE
16

© Crown Copyright 2003. All rights reserved. Licence number 0100031673

Old Wombourne Station (cafe)

The Bratch Locks

Round Oak pub

Navigation pub

Climbing to the rail trail from country lanes around Hinley.

northward return run, passing meadows of grazing cattle and horses. At the distinctive brickwork structures of the three locks at the Bratch, close the circuit by hopping back to the rail trail.

On the canal towpaths, please give way to other users and observe the Waterways Code, see page 11. At Bratch Locks dismount beside the moorings. Note that the anti-motorbike barriers on the towpaths are awkward at the best of times, and very hard to negotiate with trailerbikes, panniers or recumbents. These barriers occur intermittently.

Hazards don't include traffic but do include the height restriction at the start/finish car park in Wombourne. If you have bikes on the roof-rack, unload them before you park.

More generally, hazards include very low canal bridges. Also, in places where locks and bridges coincide, the towpath drops sharply directly towards the water. These take good bike control, so if in doubt dismount, and watch children closely. Also, be aware of walkers coming round blind corners.

On the rail trail there are also two sudden flights of steps. One hidden round a left-hand bend after 5km, the other after 8km approaching the Fens Pools reserve.

1 *From old Wombourne station, go south (ie left if facing from the car park) on the rail trail for 8km via Himley (passing into Dudley borough) to Pensnett. Watch for those steps down (see above).*

2 *Emerge overlooking Fens Pools. Leave the rail trail and head right, over the grassy mounds down to the nearside of Middle Pool (you can continue on the rail trail on*

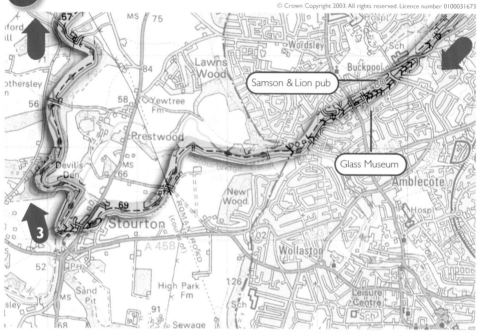

Samson & Lion pub

Glass Museum

a high embankment between Fens Pool on the left and Middle Pool on the right, and then ride all round Fens Pool). Continue round Middle Pool, then, at a gravelled car park, take the lower of two trails, with the third lake, Grove Pool, on your right. The trail turns southwest beside Wide Waters, the end of the Fens branch of the Stourbridge Canal which was restored recently. Continue along the towpath for 6km via the 16-lock flight (Samson & Lion pub) and Wordsley Junction, to the T-junction with the Staffordshire & Worcestershire Canal at Stourton.

3 Cross on the bridge and turn right, north, on the Staffordshire & Worcestershire Canal towpath. Continue for 10km, along fine stretches of peaceful canal via Greensforge Wharf, Hinksford (the Navigation pub), as far as the distinctive Bratch Locks. Turn right at the road. The rail trail bridge lies 300m ahead and, with luck, the cafe will still be open.

A flight of 16 locks, the cone of the glass museum and the Samson and Lion pub make the Stourbridge canal a real draw.

The Stourbridge Canal is particularly
picturesque, with many interesting features.

Valley Park to Womburne rail trail and canal tour

Rail trail outward – tea on the platform of old Wombourne station – canal homeward. Here's a peaceful car-free route through urban Wolverhampton and South Staffordshire countryside.

Wolverhampton Council has nurtured the old railway line on its western outskirts, naming it the Valley Park Path, elevating it to a nature reserve and giving it a visitor

centre in old Tettenhall station. To the south, after the trail crosses the county boundary, it becomes the South Staffordshire railway walk.

A mountain bike is the beast of choice for this route, and an essential after wet weather. From a civilized start at Aldersley Leisure Village (home to the Wolverhampton Wheelers with a 460m cycle track and a

RIDE INFORMATION

Distance   18km (11¼ miles)
Car-free   17.7km (11 miles) (98%)
Grade   Easy-moderate

Suitability for children and occasional riders?
OK, as long as children have very good bike control and are safe riding on the waterway – ramps are steep beside several locks. The route is flat all the way and you can turn round at Wombourne station and come back directly on the rail trail if you want to. On the canal, watch the low bridges and brick ramps.

Traffic
Zilch, other than a 300m road link from the rail trail at Wombourne station to the canal at the Bratch.

Start/finish
Start either at Aldersley Leisure Village (2km

northwest of Wolverhampton centre), next to the Aldersley cycle track, where there are parking and refreshments, or at Wombourne station, for the parking and cafe (height restriction at the entrance).

Stations
Wolverhampton is the closest, 2.5km as the crow flies from the start at Aldersley Leisure Village.

Refreshments
Aldersley Leisure Village (open all day) has a bar with food which is open from 6pm (also Weds and Fri lunchtimes); cafe at old Wombourne station; the Bridge 59 pub at Compton.

What to see
The Valley Park Nature Reserve Visitor Centre at old Tettenhall station (tel: 01902 552351).

The start of the route follows the rail trail from Aldersley
Leisure Village, where you should also try out the cycle track.

Below: Only ghost trains now run through old Wombourne
Station – where tea is served on the platform.

cyclo-cross circuit), the trail runs through
cuttings and over embankments, as you leave
the buildings behind and traverse open fields.
The turnaround point at old Wombourne
station is perfect with its cake and cuppa
formula. You are asked to dismount at the
locks at the Bratch on the Staffordshire &
Worcestershire Canal, with its neatly restored
brickworks and watercourses.

The northward return run up the canal is
tranquil – and in fact easier going than the
rail trail (which gets waterlogged after heavy
rain). Hop from the towpath back on to the
rail trail 1.5km south of the starting point,
where the old line goes over the top of it.
Wombourne old station is also the start/finish
point for the Kingswinford and Stourbridge
circuit (see Route 16).

Observe the Waterways Code on page 11.
Dismount at Bratch Locks moorings. Note that
the anti-motorbike barriers on the towpaths
are awkward at the best of times, and very
hard to negotiate with trailerbikes, panniers or
recumbents. These barriers occur intermittently.

1 *From Aldersley Leisure Village car park, the
Valley Park Path rail trail heads off south
by the exit (Hugh Porter Way). Continue for a
total of 8km, as far as old Wombourne station
(cafe).*

*Features en route include; after 1km the
nature reserve visitor centre at Tettenhall old
station; after 1.5km, the railway bridge over the
canal and Smestow Brook.*

2 *At the old station at Wombourne, leave
the rail trail left and head down to the
road. Turn right beneath the bridge, and after
300m, cross the canal. Turn right, north, on the
towpath (walk the bike by the locks), on the
Staffordshire & Worcestershire Canal. Continue
for 8km, to where you meet the rail trail again
(500m beyond Compton Lock) on the bridge
over the canal (the path to the trail lies on the
left a little before the bridge).*

3 *Turn left, north, and retrace your steps
on the rail trail back to Aldersley
Leisure Village.*

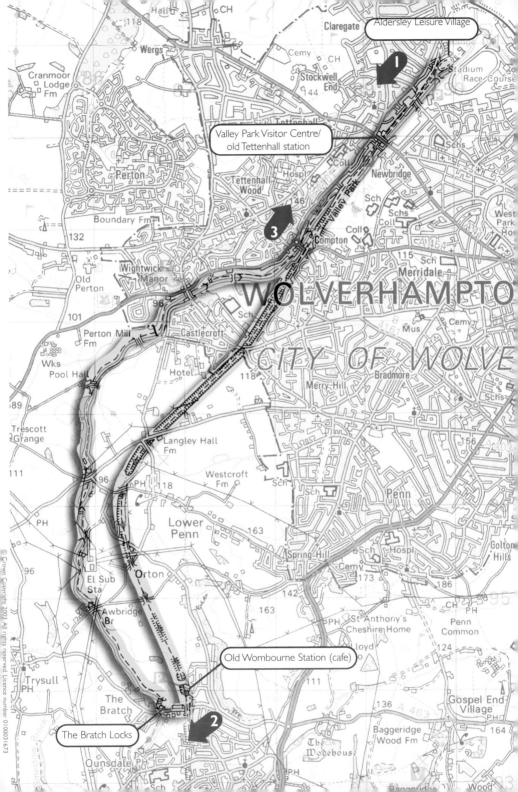

Claregate

Aldersley Leisure Village

Valley Park Visitor Centre/
old Tettenhall station

Old Wombourne Station (cafe)

The Bratch Locks

North Wolverhampton green circuit

A green and low-traffic tour of towpaths and open spaces north of the city, starting at a cycling venue and passing Moseley Old Hall, where Charles II hid after the Battle of Worcester.

Seventy per cent car-free, this circuit starts from Aldersley, passes within 1.5km of Wolverhampton centre and out round the city's northern edge. It features spectacular long views into Staffordshire from the summit of Bushbury Hill (184m), visits a historic manor house and has 6.5km of pleasant towpath riding.

We set out from Aldersley Leisure Village (home cycle stadium and cyclo-cross circuit of the Wolverhampton Wheelers) and pick up the Birmingham Main Line Canal at Aldersley Junction. We follow that southeast

RIDE INFORMATION

Distance 14.5km (9 miles)
Car-free 10km (6¼ miles) (70%)

Grade
Moderate. Several tracks are rough, and there is good climb up Bushbury Hill (184m). One section of towpath through Fordbridges near the end is rideable but narrow.

Suitability for children and occasional riders?
See Grade. Children need to have good bike control to be safe on the towpaths, and there is a tough off-road climb, also a long on-road rise. Everyone has to walk on the footpath round the busy A449/M54 roundabout.

Traffic
There are two road sections: on low-traffic, cycle-routed roads up and over Low Hill,

and on the north side of the route where you need to walk on pavement for 200m on the dual carriageway A449, and round the roundabout interchange with the M54.

Start/finish
Aldersley Leisure Village car park (2km northwest of Wolverhampton centre), Northycote Farm Country Park (just east of Bushbury, parking and cafe with height restriction on the entrance), or Moseley Old Hall car park (signed off the A449 near the M54).

Stations
Wolverhampton lies 1km south of the Fox's Lane Bridge (point 2) on the route, the closest to the city centre, where we turn off the canal and head for Low Hill.

Refreshments
Aldersley Leisure Village (tel: 01902 556200,

Heading towards Wolverhampton
on the Main Line canal.

has vending machines and a bar open
from 6pm and at lunchtimes Wed
and Fri); at Moseley Old Hall there is a
tearoom in the 18th-century barn
(which you can visit without paying to
see the house).

What to see
Moseley Old Hall (open Easter-October,
National Trust, entrance £4.20, tel: 01902
782808) is an Elizabethan house
remodelled in the 19th century, to which
King Charles escaped in 1651 following
defeat by the Roundheads.

Literature
Wolverhampton Council has a map of
the cycling network showing on and off-
road routes, available from the Road
Safety Unit, Heantun House, Salop St,
Wolverhampton WV3 0SQ
(tel: 01902 555734).

for 1.5km to Fowlers Park (the closest point
to the city centre), then take a cycle route
through the park and on roads through Low
Hill to Bushbury Hill. The track leads to the
top of the rural rise with long vistas, and the
downhill is the best in the book, but watch
for other users! A quick spin round the
perimeter of Northycote Farm Country Park
(where there's a public farm and cafe) leads to
the lanes near Moseley Old Hall, which also
has a tearoom.

The start of the return portion follows
roads briefly, and later unfortunately, requires
you to walk around a major roundabout
(although that is little bother) to pick up the
Staffordshire & Worcestershire Canal at
Coven Heath. Heading south on the towpath,
a short section around Forster Bridge is
uncomfortably narrow (but can be avoided).
Past canalside lawns, continue past Autherley
Junction back to Aldersley Junction and the
sports centre.

Tracks over Bushbury Hill, through
Northycote Farm Country Park and down
the Staffordshire & Worcestershire Canal are
too rough for a road bike – and the descent
off Bushbury is a screamer. So use a bike with

knobblies, or wait until it is dry and pump those tyres hard!

Give way to other people on the towpaths, and observe the Waterways Code (see page 11). Note that the anti-motorbike barriers on the towpaths are awkward at the best of times, and very hard to negotiate with trailerbikes, panniers or recumbents. These barriers occur intermittently.

1 *From Aldersley Leisure Centre car park, ride along by the five-aside pitches, turn right at the end over playing fields (with Wolves Football Academy on the left) and through to the canals at Aldersley Junction down on the right. Go over Aldersley Bridge, and turn off left (where the bench is on the corner) up what is the Main Line Canal, heading southeast (this is also part of the National Cycle Network). Continue for 1.5km (rising with 11 of Wolverhampton's locks) to just beyond the high Stour Valley Viaduct but before the concrete chimney, at Fox's Lane Bridge.*

2 *Leave the canal left, signed for Low Hill, head through Fowler's Park and continue over the railway, crossing to the little roundabout at the Paget Arms. Take the second exit, signed for Low Hill and Bushbury Hill. At the big grassy roundabout at Low Hill, continue straight ahead for Bushbury Hill (Leacroft Avenue).*

3 *At the top, at the T-junction (Sandy Lane), continue straight over and go up the off-road track left of the school fence – a stiff 500m climb. Bushbury Hill at the top has good views left and right (west and east). Continue on the track and bend right for a fast, rough downhill (past the cemetery).*

At the bottom (Underhill Lane) go left for 400m (ignore Northycote Farm Country Park entrance) to a T-junction (Legs Lane). Turn right behind the chevrons on to Northycote Lane 'bridleway only'. After 230m, fork right on to a gravel path and continue to the lane at the end. Turn right on the lane, and soon left for Moseley Old Hall (anyone for tea?).

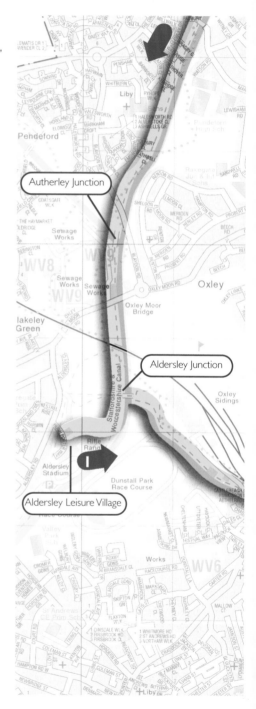

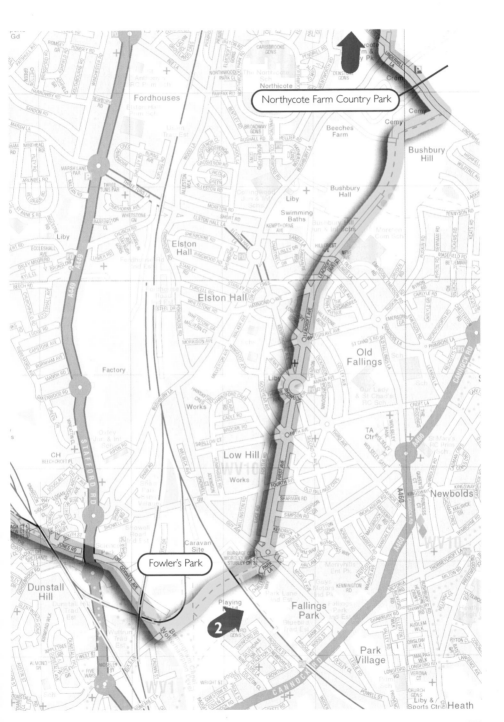

Northycote Farm Country Park

Fowler's Park

Above: The beautifully-kept Moseley Old Hall.
Below: A poplar-lined section of the
Staffordshire and Worcestershire canal.

4 Retrace your pedalstrokes and continue past where the path exits (Moseley Rd). At the junction, go right/left (Cat & Kittens Lane/Greenfield Lane) and continue in the same direction, but for this 500m section you may be better off walking on the farside pavement. At the traffic lights with the A449 dual carriageway, turn right to the roundabout interchange with the M54, and walk round on the pavement, left. On the far side, take the first left (Ball Lane) in Coven Heath. Continue to the bridge and turn left, south, on the far towpath of the Staffordshire & Worcestershire Canal.

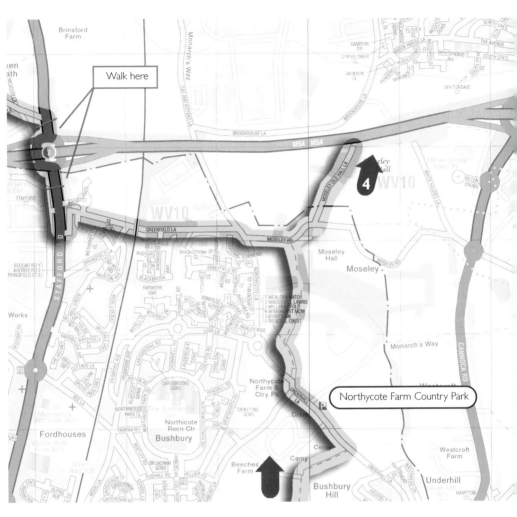

5 After 1km, the towpath becomes quite narrow close to the water's edge, although it remains rideable. To avoid this section, about 180m before the bridge take a rising forked track right off the towpath. Where the towpath disappears beside the housing, there's a tarmac track on the right. Rejoin the towpath where the surfaced path veers away to the right and continue for 1.5km (keep straight ahead at Autherly Junction, signed for Stourport) back to Aldersley Bridge. Retrace your pedalstrokes back to the sports centre car park.

Enjoy the view, then the Bushbury Hill descent.

Walsall and the Curly Wyrley

A recommended liberating route that swings between Walsall town and country on a towpath and rail trail. Start canalside at the New Art Gallery, pass restored Walsall Locks, go rural on the Wyrley & Essington Canal round Pelsall and scoot back down NCN5 directly to the heart of things.

As well as the absence of cars, the pleasures on this fine 16km tour include the Walsall New Art Gallery, the nicely restored Walsall Locks (eight in total), gorse-clad heathland north of Pelsall, and a gleeful return leg down an upgraded rail trail.

The Walsall Locks Conservation Area was created in 1987 to preserve and improve this central area. The culmination was the re-opening of the Town Arm (the starting point), now home to the steel-clad art gallery. At the

RIDE INFORMATION

Distance 16km (10 miles)
Car-free 14.4km (9 miles) (90%)

Grade
Easy-moderate (some rough towpath in the north of the route, and a section of rougher rail trail).

Suitability for children and occasional riders?
All right in dry weather. There is only 1.5km on roads through the town centre (which you can half-walk/half-ride if necessary), but children need good bike control to ride safely on 11km of towpath, including a long section which isn't surfaced. The towpath is narrow in places, and you should watch your head on the bridges.

Traffic
The town centre has a busy one-way system for 500m which involves a mid-traffic lane change (Lichfield St/Bridge St past the Town Hall). Unless you are experienced in traffic, it may be best to walk for this section, although safe cycle routeing is due in the future.

Start/finish
Start at Walsall New Art Gallery (Gallery Sq). There is parking at Crown Wharf shopping centre nearby (mind the height restriction if you have bikes on the roof); also, central town car parks (again, heed the height restriction if necessary); Birchills Canal Museum (Green St, Birchills off Old Birchills) has some street parking.

Stations
Walsall (200m from the start/finish at the New Art Gallery).

Refreshments
At the start/finish are the cafe and restaurant of the New Art Gallery, also the Wharf 10 Bar (canalside beside the art gallery) and town centre eateries; at 9.6km is Royal Oak pub on the Wyrley & Essington Canal.

What to see
The New Art Gallery (tel: 01922 654400, open Tues-Sat 10am-5pm, Sun noon-5pm,

The sleek New Art Gallery in Walsall is the start and finishing point of this route.

admission free); Birchills Canal Museum at Walsall Top Lock (tel: 01922 645778, free admission, open Tues-Wed 9.30am-12.30pm and Thurs-Sun 1pm-4pm) occupies the former Boatman's Rest Mission building. Exhibits include a walk-through narrowboat cabin and canalside relics.

Literature

An informative leaflet, the Walsall Locks Trail, about the conservation area and Birchills Canal Museum at the Top Lock is available from central tourist information. (tel: 01922 625540) or Walsall Council (tel: 01922 653116).

The West Midlands Cycle Route (NCN5) map is available from Sustrans (tel: 0117 929 0888) and shows the full linear route in detail.

The Birmingham Canal Navigations map (£4.75) is a good aid to understanding the canals (available from GeoProjects, 9 Southern Court, South St, Reading RG1 4QS, tel: 0118 939 3567).

northern extent, at the Top Lock, you will find the Birchills Canal Museum, which is also worth a visit.

The rural section of the Wyrley & Essington Canal in the north, where we traverse Pelsall Common, is probably the nicest piece of towpath riding in the book – open on both sides and grassy. Generally, the Curly Wyrley (the waterway is an early contour canal that follows the lie of the land), is a more interesting ride than straight canals. However, about halfway along, the surfacing stops and the dirt path is only suitable for sturdy bikes in the dry, and mountain bikes in the wet. In one place the path narrows to two-foot wide – anticipate and walk it if you are with unsteady riders.

The return leg runs south down the West Midlands Cycle Route (NCN5), from the outskirts of Pelsall into the heart of Walsall, mostly on a disused railway line. Future plans should include opening up more of the rail trail, possibly to give an alternative to the initial residential road section. Further south, where the NCN5 currently diverts off right for a short section, the rail trail surface is quite rough – and there's a dirt mound at the

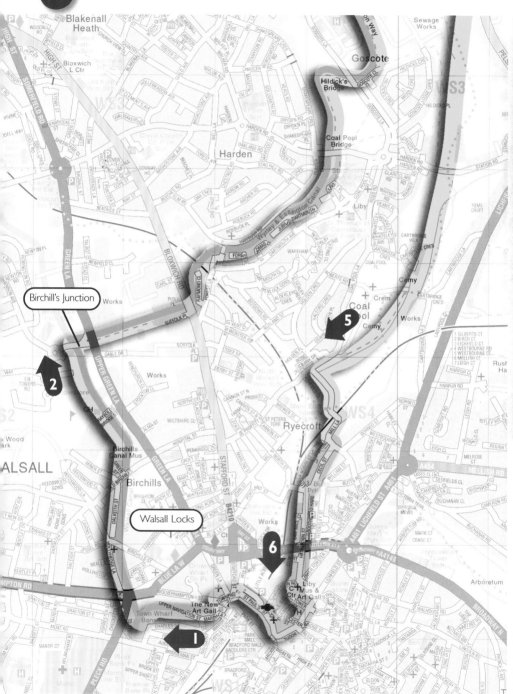

Birchill's Junction

Walsall Locks

The Curly Wyrley canal passes through the Walsall suburbs before going completely rural.

end by the toucan crossing – which may all be upgraded one day.

On the towpaths, give way to other users and follow the Waterways Code (see page 11). Note that the anti-motorbike barriers on the towpaths are awkward at the best of times, and very hard to negotiate with trailerbikes, panniers or recumbents. These barriers occur intermittently.

1 *Start at the New Art Gallery (Walsall town centre, at the end of the Town Arm Canal). Take the towpath along the Town Arm (the canal on your right, south side) for 400m to Walsall Canal Junction. Follow the towpath up and over the bridge and go right, up towards the locks (the waterway on your right). Continue*

alongside the locks (past the top lock and Birchills Canal Museum) and continue for 1km to Birchills Junction.

2 *Go over the bridge and right (the canal now on your left) to join the Wyrley & Essington Canal. Continue on the towpath for 9km, as far as High Bridge (200m before High Bridge Bridge – if you arrive at the bridge, retrace your steps).*

En route: there is a good surface for 4km to Hollands Bridge, thereafter it is a dirt track; at 7.5km, Pelsall Junction (connecting with the Cannock Extension Canal), continue in the same direction; at 8km, find the canalside Royal Oak pub.

The canal and heathland scene at the north end of the route, passing through Pelsall Common.

3 Turn right on the surfaced path which turns off the canal beside housing, NCN5 signed Timberland Trail. This runs mostly through residential roads for 1.5km to pick up the rail trail – follow signs to Walsall all the way, or use the following directions:
Continue round the right-hand bend, and then go over the little road. At Fairburn Crescent, dogleg right/left into St Paul's Crescent. (Eventually, the rail trail may go straight through from Fairburn Crescent to St Andrew's Avenue.)
   At the T-junction, turn left (St Andrew's Avenue). After 200m, turn left into Shireview Rd. At the next T-junction turn left, and go as far as the T-junction with Railswood Drive where you turn right. At the main road T-junction, turn left into Victoria Rd and almost immediately left again into Station Rd. After 350m, leave the road, heading left on the track to the rail trail.

4 Turn right along the NCN5 rail trail signed for Walsall. Continue for 3km as far as Mill Lane. En route at 800m, either follow NCN5 right around housing for 600m, or continue on the rough but rideable track in the same direction; at 2km at the cemetery, continue in the same direction on the narrow low-grade tarmac footpath.

5 At Mill Lane, continue on roads following the NCN5 for 1.5km, all the way into the centre of Walsall, ignoring the off-road tracks ahead. En route: at Mill Lane turn left, after 400m turn right into Cecil St, and at the end right/left into Hatherton St, then, at crossroads (Littleton St) keep straight ahead as far as the redbrick church. Go over the crossing, dismount and walk straight ahead (the church on your left) into Darwall St. At the end (beside the Civic Centre), turn left into the one-way system (Tower St).

6 At the end of Tower St, turn right carefully into Lichfield St past the Town Hall (casual riders/children should dismount and walk on the pavement for 200m, although dedicated cycle routeing is due). At the lights after 200m, continue into Bridge St (the main shopping street is at 2 o'clock) and leave the NCN at this point. Turn right at the square (the old clock and sculpture) into St Paul's St, round past the bus station and college, heading to the end at Townend St. Turn left – the art gallery is just round the corner.

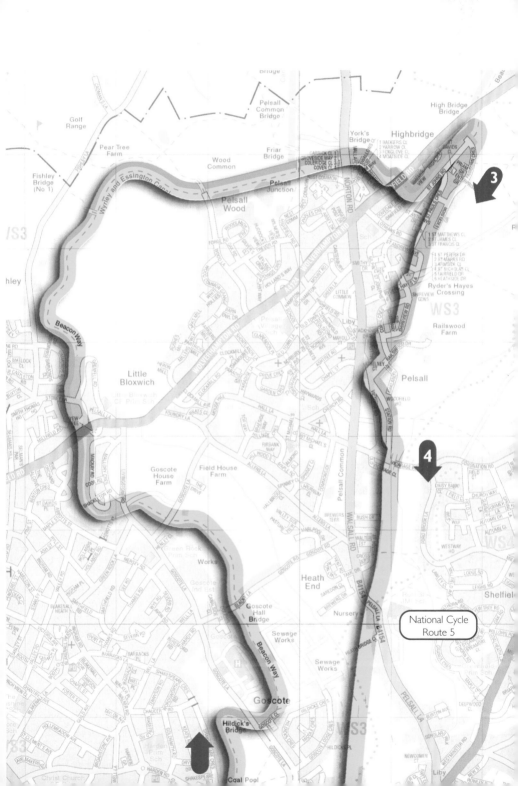

National Cycle
Route 5

Barr Beacon and the Rushall and Daw End Canals

Jump between lookout point and towpath east of Walsall on a mix of roads.

At 227m, Barr Beacon is one of the highest points in the West Midlands. On the summit a war memorial and playground yield long views west and east. Heather has been replanted to restore heathland on what is a sandstone ridge. A beacon was lit here in 1588 to celebrate the defeat of the Spanish Armada. One was lit again in 1897 to mark Queen

RIDE INFORMATION

Distance	13.5km (8½ miles)
Off-road	6.4km (4 miles) (47%)
Grade	Moderate (the towpath is unsurfaced, and there's a 60m climb back up to Barr Beacon).

Suitability for children and occasional riders?
No. The roads are too busy for children, and the climb isn't fun for pootling cyclists.

Traffic
Unfortunately, the only way to connect Barr Beacon and the Rushall Canal is on the road. On the return leg these are busy with traffic.

Start/finish
At two points; Barr Beacon – parking at either the main or north car park (off the B4154 Beacon Rd south of Aldridge), and beside the canal 1.25km northeast of Walsall at Daw End/Park Lime Pits Local Nature Reserve (reached from Daw End Lane, past the Boathouse pub) down Park Rd.

Stations
Walsall (6.4km west), Sutton Coldfield (6.4km east).

Refreshments
None on Barr Beacon but there is the canalside Boathouse pub at Daw End Bridge 4.5km along the towpath.

What to see
Barr Beacon memorial and views (countryside rangers tel: 01922 459813); Hay Head Nature Reserve, just off-route at Longwood Junction, is an old canal basin and lime works that has been reclaimed by nature.

Literature
Walsall Council (tel: 0121 360 9464) produces a good free map of Barr Beacon, featuring the panoramic views, the nature trail and historical details. The council has also produced a leaflet for Park Lime Pits and Hay Head Wood nature reserves.

The Birmingham Canal Navigations map is a good aid to understanding the canals (available from GeoProjects, 9 Southern Court, South St, Reading RG1 4QS, tel: 0118 939 3567).

If you're quick, the rainbow over the Rushall
canal may still be there . . .

Victoria's Diamond Jubilee, and once more in 1988 on the 400th anniversary of the Armada's defeat.

In the the valley to the west lies a peaceful waterway, the Rushall Canal. En route, this becomes the Daw End Branch of the 'Curly Wyrley', the Wyrley and Essington contour canal which follows the lie of the land. This route links the highpoint and waterway, but doesn't feature a great amount of picturesque riding. Riding pleasure is also affected by the fact that the towpath is unsurfaced, so after wet weather it becomes intermittently waterlogged.

From the beacon, down agricultural lanes and along the canal, things are fine. The waterway is scenic in parts, particularly after the first all-straight 1.5km on the Rushall Canal to Longwood Bridge and Junction, continuing on the Daw End Branch via Riddian Bridge into Aldridge.

The 3km from the towpath back up to the Beacon have little going for them, following first residential roads then the busy narrowing B4154 Beacon Road – and climbing all the way.

One school of thought suggests you retrace your steps from the waterside Boathouse pub at Daw End (a little over halfway round) back to the beacon, to avoid the road riding. If you do this, you must surmount Barr Beacon via the North car park – see direction 4 (the road you descend off the ridge is one-way); back at the top of the lanes go left at Beacon Rd, and dismount to go right (dangerous in this narrow, busy road) after 300m up into the Beacon area.

This ride isn't for children (unless you simply pootle around on the top of the beacon, or retrace from the Boathouse pub), but will suit cyclists who are comfortable in traffic – and whose bikes can cope with a rather unpredictable towpath.

On the towpath give way to other users and follow the Waterways Code, see page 11. Note that the anti-motorbike barriers on the towpaths are awkward at the best of times, and very hard to negotiate with trailerbikes, panniers or recumbents. These occur intermittently.

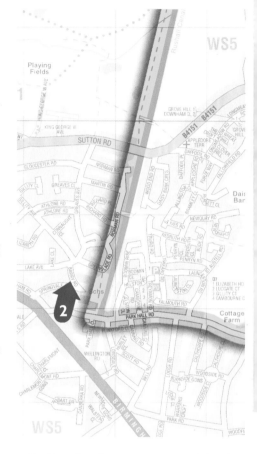

1 From Barr Beacon main car park, head north past the war memorial and down the steep tarmac exit road to the main Beacon Road (B4154). With care, go right on the road and soon turn left, downhill on a lane. After 400m, turn right by a white farmhouse (Bodens Lane). At the T-junction after 500m, turn left (Crook Lane). After 400m, turn right into Barr Lakes Lane, and after 800m go left again on to a busier lane (Skip Lane). At the T-junction at the end, turn right into residential Park Hall Rd and continue for 800m to the canal bridge.

2 Turn right on the Rushall Canal towpath, with the canal on your right. Continue for 6.5km (pass Rushall Top Lock/Longwood Junction after 3km, Riddian Bridge after 3.5km, and the

Below: Twilight brings a stillness to the waters of the Daw End canal beneath the Riddian Bridge.

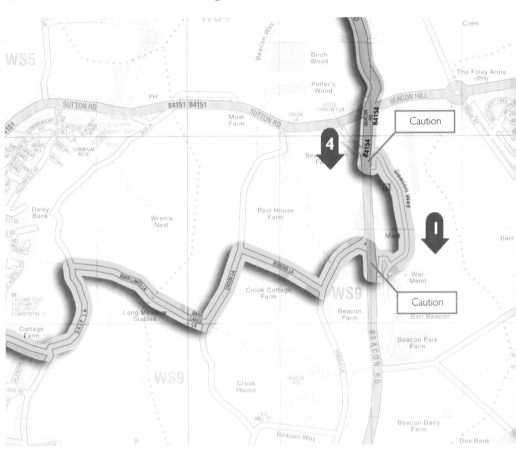

Above: Atop Barr Beacon (227m), a good place to catch the sun and the wind, and the route's start/finish point. Below: Woops, too late!

Boathouse pub after 4.5km). Leave the towpath at Hopleys Bridge/Dumblederry Lane.

3 Turn right on the road bridge over the canal, Dumblederry Lane/Paddock Lane, and continue 1km to the crossing with the A454, Walsall Lane. Go carefully straight ahead into Tyning's Lane. At the end, turn right into Birmingham Rd. At the end, turn left joining busy, rising Barr Common. After 400m, turn right

carefully into Longwood Rd, becoming Beacon Rd after 1km at traffic lights. Ride carefully on this narrow section.

4 After 250m, turn left up the steep tarmac road to Barr Beacon North car park. At the top, continue on the track in the same direction, and follow beside the underground reservoir. At the end, cross the field back to the war memorial and the main car park.

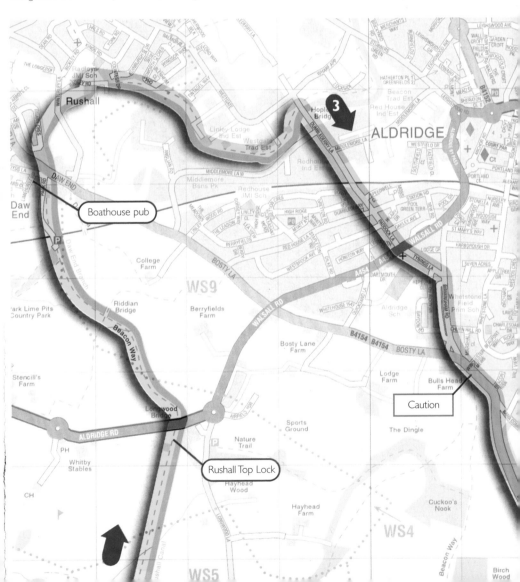

ACKNOWLEDGEMENTS

Birmingham City Council

Thanks go to the following for their invaluable help in working out the routes in this book:

Dan Barnett, countryside sites officer, Worcestershire County Council (Waseley Hills)
Lydia Barnstable, Wolverhampton Council
Simon Cooper, area parks manager,
Michael Groll and Mike Paley, Push Bikes
(the Birmingham cycling campaign)
Sally Hamlyn and Nick Ireland, British Waterways, Birmingham & Black Country
Joe Hayden, head ranger, Lickey Hills
Anthea Jones, Walsall Council
Graham Lennard, Birmingham Council
Don MacDougall, Dudley Council
John McIlroy, Sandwell Council
Jayne Ogilvie, Sustrans
John Porter, head ranger, Sutton Park
Sam Purchase, Solihull Council
Liz Stuffins and Eric Clarke, Walsall Countryside Services

Thanks also to Gary and Trish Hooper and Mandy Ross for local pointers and hospitality, and Judith Foster for logistics.

Author	**Nicky Crowther**
Project Manager	**Louise McIntyre**
Editor	**Peter Nicholson**
Design	**Simon Larkin**
Page Layout	**Chris Fayers**
	James Robertson
Photography	**Nicky Crowther**
Front Cover photo	**Mike Paley**
Clent Hills photos	**Colin MacDonald**
	www.stourbridge.com

Mapping reproduced from Philip's Birmingham Street Atlas © Philip's 2003 Cartography by Philip's
This product includes mapping data licensed from Ordnance Survey ® with the permission of the Controller of Her Majesty's Stationary Office.
© Crown copyright 2003. All rights reserved. Licence number 100011710.

Ordnance Survey Landranger (rides 16 and 17) and Explorer (ride 12) maps supplied by Emapsite.com.
© Crown Copyright 2003. All rights reserved.
Licence number 0100031673.